AF412454

Symbol and Empowerment

Symbol and Empowerment:
Paul Tillich's
Post-Theistic System

Richard Grigg

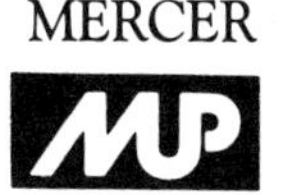

Symbol and Empowerment
Copyright © 1985
Mercer University Press, Macon GA 31207
All rights reserved
Printed in the United States of America

Library of Congress Cataloging in Publication Data
Grigg, Richard, 1955–
Symbol and empowerment.

Bibliography: p. 133
Includes index.
1. Tillich, Paul, 1886–1965. 2. Symbolism—History—
20th century. I. Title.
BX4827.T53G75   1985   230'.092'4   85-7214
ISBN 0-86554-163-9 (alk. paper)

Contents

Acknowledgments

vii

Introduction

ix

1
The Fundamental Tenets
of Tillich's Theology
and Their Implications
for Religious Symbolism

1

2
The Nature of Symbols

31

3
Correlation
as a Hermeneutical Method

53

4
Symbol,
Empowerment,
and the World Religions
105

Conclusion
129

Bibliography
133

Index
149

Acknowledgments

Special thanks to
Robert P. Scharlemann
for his invaluable advice.

Introduction

In Langdon Gilkey's contribution to the new edition of *The Theology of Paul Tillich*, he mentions a curious fact about Tillich's present standing in the theological world. On the one hand, "while many of the great theological systems of the first half of this century are now more of historical than contemporary interest, Tillich's is one with which we continue to wrestle." Tillich "remains in the forefront of our intellectual scene as a massive and widespread influence pervading and reshaping much of our thinking." Yet, on the other hand, "as many observers have remarked, there is no Tillichian 'school'; that is, a self-conscious community of thinkers who pattern their thought on his."[1] Although it is likely the situation described has a number of causes, there is one characteristic of Tillich's thought that can be singled out as a factor in both his continuing influence and his lack of a school following: Paul Tillich has worked out a detailed post-theistic interpretation of the Christian faith. In his *Systematic Theology*, which will be the focus of this study, Tillich shows how the Christian concept of God can be seen as a symbol for a reality ontologically more fundamental than the Supreme Being, the apparent referent of the concept of God if that concept is taken literally. The attractiveness of Tillich's "God above the God of theism"[2] and hence Tillich's enduring influence

---

[1]Langdon Gilkey, "Tillich: The Master of Mediation," in *The Theology of Paul Tillich*, 2d ed., ed. Charles W. Kegley (New York: Pilgrim Press, 1982) 26.

[2]See Paul Tillich, *The Courage to Be* (New Haven: Yale University Press, 1952) 182-90.

within the theological world are understandable in light of the problems—
recognized since Kant—that many philosophers and religious thinkers believe accompany the claim that God exists as a Supreme Being.

What, then, in Tillich's post-theistic system works against his gain-
ing a school following? While the general direction of Tillich's transcendence of theism is attractive to many, it is possible that some of the details
of his system are not. Tillich equates his God-above-the-God-of-theism
with being-itself, and his notion of being-itself seems to be rooted in the
world view created by nineteenth-century German idealists such as Schelling and Hegel.[3] Many contemporary theologians, especially those predis-
posed to the Anglo-American philosophical tradition, feel more
comfortable with the categories employed by a Lonergan or a Whitehead
than with something like Tillich's being-itself.

It is my contention that what I shall call the "phenomenon of empowerment" is a crucial component of Tillich's post-theistic system. Exploring its role in the *Systematic Theology* can reveal the experiential basis
of Tillich's discussion of being-itself and thereby clarify Tillichian forms
of thought and expression that may seem strange to those not at home in
the world of nineteenth-century German philosophy. Furthermore, such
an exploration can uncover the connection between being-itself and religious symbols that allows Tillich to reinterpret the essential elements of
the Christian tradition in a post-theistic fashion.

Reference to empowerment as a "phenomenon" is meant to emphasize its being a matter of human consciousness and not of causal processes

---

[3]For example, on p. 179 of *The Courage to Be*, Tillich describes being-itself
in terms of the "negation of the negation of being." At various points in his writings, he does deal explicitly with his debt to German idealism. See, for example,
"On the Boundary between Idealism and Marxism," trans. N. A. Rasetzki, in *The
Interpretation of History* (New York: Scribner's, 1936) 60-67. Compare his ad-
vocacy of a "self-transcending realism" in "Realism and Faith," trans. James Luther Adams, in *The Protestant Era*, abridged ed., ed. James Luther Adams
(Chicago: University of Chicago Press, 1957) 66-82. Regarding Tillich's vacil-
lation between idealism and realism in the actual working out of his theology, see
p. 188 of John Herman Randall's "The Ontology of Paul Tillich," in *The Theology of Paul Tillich.*

external to consciousness.[4] While the object of one's consciousness can be something external to consciousness, one's empowerment by that object is a result of events occurring *within* consciousness; empowerment is a function of how one thinks that object. The phenomenon of empowerment is the experience of being enabled to overcome a conflict between a goal and a barrier within oneself to reaching that goal. Empowerment is, in other words, a three-part dialectic. First, one has an identity goal, a desire to become the sort of person one believes one should be but presently is not. It is a matter of one's *being*, when being is understood as one's *existence* plus the *meaning* of one's existence.[5] Second, one finds oneself unable to attain one's identity goal, not because of external circumstances, but because of a resistance as much a part of one's own disposition as the goal it conflicts with. In the third stage of the dialectic, the resistance is overcome, and one finds oneself able to attain one's goal. This third stage is experienced as empowerment because it comes from outside oneself as one is defined by the conflict between goal and resistance. But it is empowering as a new dimension of consciousness, not as a power external to consciousness.

What empowerment is may be further clarified by considering four imaginary cases. The first three cases are *not* examples of empowerment; the last one *is*.

1. I wish to fly from Chicago to New York, but a snowstorm between the two cities foils my plans. Subsequently, I discover that I can fly from Chicago to Charleston, West Virginia, and from there to New York; I thereby fly around the storm.

2. Because I am concerned about my health, I want to give up my habit of smoking cigarettes, but I am unable to do so. I go to a doctor who prescribes a drug that suppresses my craving for nicotine, and I quit smoking.

---

[4]The association of the word *phenomenon* with consciousness is due primarily to the work of the European "phenomenological" school, whose best-known representative is Edmund Husserl. According to Tillich, consciousness is one of the fundamental poles presupposed in one's experiencing anything at all, the other pole being the objective pole, the world. See *Systematic Theology*, 3 vols. (Chicago: University of Chicago Press, 1951-1963) 1:164; hereafter cited as *ST*.

[5]See ibid., 14.

3. On Monday morning, John says something to me that angers me.
    All day I tell myself that I ought to overcome my anger against John,
    but I am unable to bring myself to forgive him. When I wake up
    Tuesday morning, however, I discover that my anger has subsided.

Why do none of these cases exemplify empowerment? The first case involves a conflict occurring not within the self but between a goal and external circumstances. What is more, the goal is not an identity goal.

The second case fails because, while the conflict is indeed a conflict
within the self, the resolution is not itself a function of consciousness but
of a causal sequence external to consciousness.

The third case fails because the three-part dialectic is not present. If
the resolution is not experienced as appearing over against a genuine conflict within the self, then it is not experienced as empowering. In this case,
the resolution occurs only because the resistance to what the person wanted
to accomplish disappears.

What case would exemplify the phenomenon of empowerment?

4. Suppose that when I am quite young, I set my heart on becoming
    a surgeon. When the time comes, I enter medical school and from
    medical school proceed to surgical residency. The residency turns
    out to be more difficult than I had imagined. I am expected to work
    extraordinarily long hours, and I get little sleep. Soon I find myself
    tempted to give up. At that point, in the face of the conflict be-
    tween my great desire to become a surgeon and my temptation to
    quit, I envision what it would be like to finish the residency and
    become a practicing surgeon. I think about the feeling of accom-
    plishment, about the prestige and the excitement. Perhaps I even
    incorporate these ideas into concrete images. These images prod
    me to go on, to recommit myself to attaining the goal I have set for
    myself. I may use such images self-consciously as a device. In other
    words, every time I am tempted to give up, I call the images to mind,
    making them just as detailed and vivid as I can.

In this fourth case, the conflict takes place within the self, the goal is, at
least indirectly, an identity goal, the resolution is a function of consciousness, and the three parts of the dialectic are present. To self-consciously
use an image or idea as a device for self-motivation is no doubt a common
practice, and it is a practice dependent on the empowering quality of an
image or idea.

The relevance of the phenomenon of empowerment for the theological tradition Paul Tillich is situated in lies in Christianity's view of the human self as divided against itself. As William James puts it in his classic study *The Varieties of Religious Experience*, one's inner being "is a battleground for what he feels to be two deadly hostile selves, one actual, the other ideal."[6] The apostle Paul's cry describes the situation perfectly:

> I can will what is right, but I cannot do it. For I do not do the good I want, but the evil I do not want is what I do. . . . I delight in the law of God, in my inmost self, but I see in my members another law at war with the law of my mind and making me captive to the law of sin which dwells in my members. Wretched man that I am! Who will deliver me from this body of death?[7]

Paul's quest for deliverance is a quest for empowerment, for the power to overcome the conflict between his desire to become the person he believes he ought to be and his inner resistance to that desire.[8]

The type of empowerment, or deliverance, manifest in Christianity is usually interpreted, at least by Christians, as coming from outside the one empowered. If one returns to case 4, that of the person who wants to become a surgeon, and one tries to locate the source of that person's empowerment, one might conclude that it is a clarification of his own, already existing identity goal that leads to empowerment. That is, by envisioning all the implications of his identity goal, he overcomes the temptation to turn away from it. How does Christianity's view of empowerment differ? Christian theologians speak of an empowerment that results from the grace of God. They often claim that only through divine agency can one overcome the kind of inner conflict Paul speaks of. However, while the empowerment involved here is said to depend upon a reality outside the person empowered, the phenomenon itself still takes place

---

[6]William James, *The Varieties of Religious Experience* (New York: The New American Library, 1958) 143. Note that Lecture 8 in James's book is entitled "The Divided Self, and the Process of its Unification."

[7]Romans 7:18b-24. Revised Standard Version. The National Council of the Churches of Christ, 1946.

[8]A disciple of Martin Luther might suggest that what is required here is not empowerment but forensic justification. But see below, chap. 3, n. 48.

within consciousness. This situation is especially evident in those cases where God's grace is said to empower the believer indirectly. The Christ-event, for example, is sometimes said to be the manifestation of God's grace; one is empowered to overcome self-conflict when one appropriates the good news of that event on faith. One then understands one's identity in a new light: one's being is given to one by God, and is not attained by "good works." But even in a case in which God is seen as empowering someone more directly, if human freedom is to be seen as truly enabled or empowered and not simply abrogated, God's grace must be seen as working within the context of that person's consciousness.

The view of the phenomenon of empowerment in Tillich's *Systematic Theology* originates in the Christian tradition. Tillich's version of empowerment, too, looks to a reality outside the self. Indeed, it looks to a reality he calls "God." But Tillich is true to his post-theistic commitment, and empowerment as he describes it bears the marks of that commitment. In the form of empowerment that appears in Tillich's *Systematic Theology*, the conflict to be overcome is constituted by a tension between two fundamental poles of the ontological structure as that structure is given to consciousness.

Chapter 1 will explore the premises of Tillich's ontology and theology and their implications for religious symbolism. Empowerment will play an important role here, for, given these premises, the experience of religious empowerment establishes the reality of what Tillich terms "being-itself."

Chapter 2 will deal with the details of Tillich's theory of religious symbols. Empowerment will be discussed with respect to both the characteristics and truth of these symbols.

Chapter 3 will investigate Tillich's "method of correlation" as it pertains to the interpretation of religious symbols. I shall suggest that one can distinguish between the explicit apologetic function of the method of correlation and an implicit hermeneutical function. Here too the phenomenon of empowerment will be central, for I shall argue that empowerment provides a datum without which the correlation attempted by Tillich cannot succeed.

Chapter 4 will apply the discoveries of the first three chapters in a way that goes beyond what Tillich undertakes in the *Systematic Theology*: I shall attempt to show how one might construct a Tillichian "world theology." Here it will become evident, I hope, that Tillich's unique brand of post-theistic religious thought can be a basis for a theology embracing all of the world's major religions.

The study concludes with a consideration of the implications of the central role given to empowerment in Tillich's post-theistic system. Tillich's description of God as being-itself, rather than as the Supreme Being, draws upon a vocabulary and a group of concepts associated with post-Kantian idealism. But if the experience of empowerment is the foundation for Tillich's discussion of being-itself, his post-theistic interpretation of Christian belief is less dependent upon German idealism than it first appears. Thus, if one were to focus upon the phenomenon of empowerment, one might be able to appropriate the post-theistic component of Tillich's system and apply it within the context of philosophies different from the one suggested by Tillich's own vocabulary. In the Conclusion, I shall take a brief look at this possibility.

1

The Fundamental Tenets
of Tillich's Theology
and Their Implications
for Religious Symbolism

According to many twentieth-century thinkers, Paul Tillich among them, symbols play an essential role in religion. However, when Tillich makes that statement, he bases it upon the fundamental tenets of his own unique theological position. In this chapter, I shall attempt to uncover the connections between the major premises of Tillich's theology and the place given to symbolism in that theology. This will require an examination of what Tillich considers a more purely philosophical dimension of his thought—namely, his ontological analysis—and an examination of his notion of religion.

Ontology and Being-itself

I have suggested that the phenomenon of empowerment can be shown to have a central place in Tillich's system. Furthermore, empowerment is to be understood as taking place within consciousness. Thus, it should be unsurprising that, in the exposition that follows, I have chosen to emphasize that Tillich's ontology is truly *phenomenological*. In other words, the

manner in which reality is given to human consciousness, far from being
a barrier to an accurate description of what is real, is itself a constitutive
element of reality. When "man" seeks to understand the nature of being,
he turns first to his own being, for

> he has become aware of the fact that he himself is the door to the deeper
> levels of reality, that in his own existence he has the only possible ap-
> proach to existence itself. [Here Tillich adds the following footnote: "Cf.
> Augustine's doctrine of truth dwelling in the soul and transcending it
> at the same time; the mystical identification of the ground of being with
> the ground of self; the use of psychological categories for ontological
> purposes in Paracelsus, Böhme, Schelling, and in the 'philosophy of life'
> from Schopenhauer to Bergson; Heidegger's notion of 'Dasein' (being
> there) as the form of human existence and the entrance to ontology."]
> This does not mean that man is more approachable than other objects
> as material for scientific research. The opposite is the case: It does mean
> that the immediate experience of one's own existing reveals something
> of the nature of existence generally. Whoever has penetrated into the
> nature of his own finitude can find the traces of finitude in everything
> that exists. And he can ask the question implied in his finitude as the
> question implied in finitude universally. In doing so, he does not for-
> mulate a doctrine of man; he expresses a doctrine of existence as ex-
> perienced in him as man.[1]

Tillich thus follows in the footsteps of a long line of thinkers who believe
that being is best uncovered through an investigation of "human" being.[2]

The starting point for Tillich's ontology is the phenomenon of ontological or metaphysical "shock," the shock of possible nonbeing, the rec-

---

[1]*ST,* 1:62-63.

[2]It is appropriate that Heidegger is included in Tillich's list of those who have
used human being as the point of entry into a general ontology, for Heidegger's
Being and Time, where the being of *Dasein* is taken as the fundamental clue to
the meaning of being itself, was especially influential in the development of Tillich's thought. Note that Tillich lists *Being and Time* as one of the ten books that
most shaped his vocational attitude and philosophy of life. See *Gesammelte Werke,*
14 vols., ed. Renate Albrecht (Stuttgart: Evangelische Verlagswerk, 1959-1975)
14:222.

ognition that everything that is might just as well *not* have been.[3] This shock is expressed in what Tillich terms "the ontological question":

> What is being itself? What is that which is not a special being or a group of beings, not something concrete or something abstract, but rather something which is always thought implicitly, and sometimes explicitly, if something is said to *be*?[4]

Using this "question" (which is "the expression of a state of existence rather than a formulated question"[5]) as a starting point, Tillich reconstructs the structure of being by laying out four levels of ontological concepts. Ontology, he says, uses concepts that are "less universal than being but more universal than any ontic concept, that is, more universal than any concept designating a realm of beings."[6]

The ontological question presupposes, as a condition of its possibility, a subject who questions and an object that is questioned about. This subject-object relation in turn presupposes a self-world relation. The self-world relation is the first level of the ontological structure. That Tillich begins his analysis by suggesting that because the self-world structure is presupposed in human experience all being is characterized by a self-world structure, again brings to attention that he is proceeding phenomenologically, and it suggests that his phenomenology is of a "transcendental" variety in the Kantian sense of that term.

The second level contains three pairs of polar elements: individuality and universality, dynamics and form, and freedom and destiny. The first element in each pair is directly proportional to the second element in the pair, so that as the first element is realized so is the second element realized to the same degree. Tillich states that in each of the pairs "the first element expresses the self-relatedness of being, its power of being something for itself, while the second element expresses the belongingness of being, its character of being a part of a universe of being."[7] The polar elements are

---

[3]*ST*, 1:113, 163.

[4]Ibid.

[5]Ibid., 164.

[6]Ibid.

[7]Ibid., 165.

founded upon the self-world structure of being, thereby proving themselves to be derived phenomenologically. An observation Tillich makes concerning the polarity of freedom and destiny sheds further light on his intent:

> Since freedom and destiny constitute an ontological polarity, everything that participates in being must participate in this polarity. But man, who has a complete self and a world, is the only being who is free in the sense of deliberation, decision, and responsibility. Therefore, freedom and destiny can be applied to subhuman nature only by way of analogy; this parallels the situation with respect to the basic ontological structure and the other ontological polarities.[8]

An analysis of human being describes being generally, at least in the sense that human being is analogous to the rest of being.

The third level of the ontological structure contains the conditions of "existence" and the conditions of the transition from essential to existential being. Tillich's description involves an analysis of finitude and infinity, and of how finitude relates to: freedom and destiny, being and nonbeing, and essence and existence. The phenomenological character of the investigation lies in Tillich's deriving his notion of existence from the human experience of existential estrangement; essential and existential being are juxtaposed in the same way as traditional theology juxtaposed human nature before and after the Fall.

The fourth level of the ontological structure contains the concepts of time, space, causality, and substance. Influenced by Kant, Tillich calls these concepts "categories" and describes them as "structures of finite being and thinking."[9]

With regard to these four levels, Tillich states that all ontological concepts are a priori because they are the conditions of the possibility of human experience. "Those concepts are a priori which are presupposed in every actual experience, since they constitute the very structure of experience itself."[10] The phenomenological, transcendental character of Tillich's method becomes apparent yet again.

---

[8]Ibid., 185; compare Tillich, *The Courage to Be*, 24-25.

[9]*ST*, 1:165.

[10]Ibid., 166.

While Tillich's four-level analysis of the ontological structure does flow from the ontological question, the substance of the ontological question itself appears untouched. The four levels of concepts are, after all, concepts that are "less universal than being,"[11] while the ontological question seeks being-itself. Indeed, the very nature of the ontological structure Tillich has laid out forces one to look beyond the structure, and it does so in at least three ways.

First, there is an unconditional element within the finite structure of being: this forces one to look beyond the structure. For example, the theoretical functions of reason imply an awareness of the *verum ipsum*, the true-itself as the norm of all attempts to reach the truth, and the practical functions of reason imply the reality of the *bonum ipsum*, the good-itself. The true-itself and the good-itself point one to *esse ipsum*, being-itself, which lies beyond the structure of finite being. Second, the threat of nonbeing forces one to look beyond the structure. The threat of nonbeing causes one to seek the power of being that can conquer nonbeing. It has been shown how the ontological shock, the shock of possible nonbeing, gets expressed in the ontological question that seeks being-itself. Third, the polarities that constitute the ontological structure force one to look beyond the structure. They are, according to their essence, in tension with one another, but there is danger that the unity of the elements may be destroyed. One is thus forced to search beyond the structure of being for that ground of being in which the elements are unified.[12]

In all three cases one is searching for that which negates the negation of being.[13] According to Tillich's ontology, finitude is characterized by the

---

[11]Ibid., 164.

[12]Ibid., 204-10. Tillich associates these three points of departure with three traditional arguments for the existence of God: the ontological argument, the cosmological argument, and the teleological argument. They are not valid proofs, he says, but do indicate the possibility and necessity of looking beyond the structure of finitude.

[13]Tillich, *The Courage to Be*, 179. Tillich's actual wording here is that "being must be thought as the negation of the negation of being." He does not mean that the concrete occurrence of the negation of the negation of being is being-itself. Note that Tillich understands courage as an occurrence of the negation of the negation of being and that he says, not that courage *is* being-itself, but that being-itself is the *source* of courage; see ibid., 155-56.

juxtaposition and mutual opposition of being and nonbeing: "Being, limited by nonbeing, is finitude."[14] Just as Hegel's infinite cannot stand in simple opposition to the finite (if it did it would be limited by the finite and thus would not be genuinely infinite) but stands—as the negation of the negation of the finite—in dialectical relation to the finite, so Tillich's being-itself as that which negates nonbeing's negation of being cannot exist within finitude but is that which is "beyond" the structure of finitude.

But it is difficult to conceive of a reality lying beyond the structure of finite being. In fact, such a reality is in an important sense inconceivable. If being-itself lies beyond the self-world structure of finitude, then one cannot know what it is in and of itself but only what it is not or what it is in relation to other things. Consider the three fundamental ways in which one can describe what something is.[15] First, one can employ accidental predication, exemplified by the sentence "Socrates is white." The word *white* here points to a particular characteristic Socrates possesses. No such predication can be made of being-itself, however, for being-itself is not an entity possessing certain qualities and lacking others. As that which lies beyond the self-world structure of being, being-itself is not an entity at all. The problem here lies not in a limitation of human speech but in that being-itself does not possess attributes.

One might complain that the preceding arguments contain contradictions. For example, it was said that being-itself lies beyond the self-world structure—a statement that appears to be an example of accidental predication—and then concluded that, because being-itself lies beyond the structure of being, no qualities can be predicated of it. But the statement that being-itself lies beyond the structure of being does not, in fact, provide any positive information about being-itself. Instead, it denies that certain characteristics can be applied to being-itself. Such a statement exemplifies what classical theology refers to as the *via negativa.* Similarly, the statement that being-itself negates the negation of being merely says something about how being-itself is related to the structure of finitude; it does not say what being-itself is.

---

[14]*ST*, 1:189.

[15]Compare Panayot Butchvarov, *Being Qua Being: A Theory of Identity, Existence, and Predication* (Bloomington: Indiana University Press, 1979) 1-3.

What, then, of the second way of describing what something is—essential predication—wherein a definition is provided? Here too one comes up empty-handed. Consider the statement "Man is a rational animal." It expresses the essence of man by placing man within a genus (animal) and indicating a specific difference (rationality) that pinpoints his place within that genus. But there is no genus in which one can place being-itself, for being-itself is the unconditional ground of being; there can be nothing outside it to encompass it.[16]

The third way of describing what something is, is exemplified by the statement "The morning star is the evening star." Here there is neither accidental predication nor essential predication but an identity statement. Given an identity statement, if one knows that certain qualities belong to the object mentioned in the clause that follows the word *is,* one may predicate those qualities of the subject of the sentence. Suppose that one knows nothing of the morning star, but one knows that the evening star is the planet Venus and that Venus has an average radius of 3,800 miles. Once one learns that the morning star and the evening star are identical, one can say, "The morning star has an average radius of 3,800 miles." Can one use this procedure in the case of being-itself? The obvious problem where being-itself is concerned is that because, given its nature, one can predicate no qualities of being-itself, one cannot predicate any qualities of something with which being-itself is identical.

One is thus left with only negative and relational data about being-itself. Furthermore, even the relational data is problematic. Many of the relations that Tillich claims hold between being-itself and beings (recall, for example, the statement that being-itself negates the negation of being) seem to be based upon the causal relation. But causality has been shown to be a category of finite being and thinking; it cannot be applied outside the realm of the finite. If being-itself were to become a cause, then, in the traditional view of causality, its standing vis-à-vis objects within the structure of being would be describable in terms of spatial and temporal contiguity, the temporal priority of the cause to the effect, the constant conjunction of cause and effect, and the necessary connection of cause and

---

[16]See Paul Tillich, *Love, Power, and Justice* (London: Oxford University Press, 1954) 35.

effect.[17] This description would reduce being-itself to an object standing over against other objects within the structure of being; being-itself would no longer be the unconditional ground of being. Thus, Tillich believes that the notion of causality can only be applied symbolically or metaphorically if it is to be applied to being-itself.[18] In other words, because one can think the relationship between being-itself and the structure of finite being only in terms of the categories of finite being, those categories must be used. But because the categories of finitude cannot properly be applied to being-itself, they must be understood as symbols.

Do not these arguments suggest that Tillich is on shaky ground in talking about being-itself? In what sense can the term *being-itself* be said to refer to anything if its purported referent is necessarily inconceivable, possessing no positive and nonrelational qualities? Tillich himself admits that being-itself cannot be said to "exist," for existence characterizes entities only and not the ground of being.[19] Would it not be appropriate, then, to apply Hegel's assertion that "pure Being and pure Nothing are . . . one and the same"[20] to Tillich's being-itself?

The phenomenological character of Tillich's ontology becomes crucial here, for Tillich can respond that, while being-itself cannot be conceptualized, there is a way in which it is given to consciousness. But if distinguishing qualities cannot be assigned to being-itself, it cannot be given to consciousness in any mode: a reality with no distinguishing predicates provides nothing to be conscious *of*. How can one distinguish a case in which there is an awareness of being-itself from a case in which there is not, if being-itself is such that no positive characteristics can be predicated of it?

Tillich's answer—the answer implicit in his system—takes one back to the polar structure that underlies his ontology. In certain forms of the

---

[17]Compare David Hume's famous discussion of causality in *A Treatise of Human Nature*, bk. 1, pt. 3, secs. 2, 3, 14 and 15.

[18]See *ST*, 1:237-38.

[19]See, for example, *ST*, 1:204-205.

[20]Quoted in Martin Heidegger, "What is Metaphysics?" trans. R. F. C. Hull and Alan Crick, in *Existence and Being*, ed. with introduction by Werner Brock (London: Vision Press, 1949) 377.

phenomenon of empowerment, two poles of the structure of finite being interact in such a way that a reality transcending the structure is revealed. As I shall show later, the consciousness of being-itself that comes through empowerment is, in turn, dependent upon what might be termed a "symbolic consciousness" of being-itself. A symbol of being-itself is a prerequisite for the experience of empowerment, and the symbol, too, provides an awareness of being-itself. But it is the phenomenon of empowerment that provides the richest consciousness of being-itself. Thus, empowerment would seem to provide the strongest rejoinder to those who question the reality of being-itself. For that reason I shall treat the awareness of being-itself that empowerment affords before touching upon the symbolic consciousness that makes empowerment possible. Below are three examples of empowerment, beginning with the phenomenon of courage.[21] Tillich defines finitude as being that is limited by nonbeing. This assault of nonbeing upon being is given to consciousness in the mood of anxiety, while in the mood of courage anxiety is conquered. Courage, then, is the experience of a power that overcomes a conflict within consciousness; it is an example of the phenomenon of empowerment. The conflict overcome in this case is not trivial, but one between two poles of the structure of finite being: courage is the negation of the conflict between nonbeing and being that characterizes finitude. As such, it is the manifestation to consciousness of a reality transcending the structure of finitude. "Every act of courage is a manifestation of the ground of being,"[22] for the ground of being is the "source" of courage.[23]

---

[21]The three examples that follow, the first having to do with being as it essentially ought to be, the second with being as "fallen," and the third with the ambiguous mixture of essential and "fallen" being, are taken from the three major sections of Tillich's *Systematic Theology* and will be treated in detail in chapter 3. They are actually religious phenomena, dependent upon certain religious symbols, and thus extend beyond the purely philosophical analysis undertaken so far. But inasmuch as they do tell something about the validity of the notion of being-itself, they are of philosophical interest. Tillich remarks that "the openness of being-itself, which is given in the basic religious experience, is the foundation for the philosophical grasp of the structure of being." *ST*, 1:235.

[22]Tillich, *The Courage to Be*, 181.

[23]Ibid., 156. Tillich's argument here, found also in *ST* 1 (for example, pp. 186-98, 209, 273-76), is indebted to Martin Heidegger's "What is Metaphysics?"

The second example pertains to the disruption of the polar elements of being that can occur when the essential character of the structure of being is compromised. In essential being, the polar elements are in a state of polar tension. But under certain conditions this polar unity can be destroyed. Freedom, for example, when no longer in proper tension with destiny, may degenerate into mere arbitrariness, and destiny may become mechanical necessity. But Tillich describes a phenomenon of "New Being" wherein the conflict between essential being and distorted being is overcome and the essential relationship between the two poles is restored.[24] If "New Being" exists, then one is able to experience a reality that acts not simply upon one pole or the other or upon both poles as individual components, but that manifests the essential ground in which the polar structure is rooted. Because these poles are fundamental structural components of finite being, the essential ground revealed in this phenomenon is the ground of finite being, that is, being-itself.

A third example pertains to the ambiguity Tillich sees in all forms of language. The ambiguity of language, its ability to communicate accurately something of the nature of reality and simultaneously to obscure the true nature of reality, is due to the subject-object cleavage upon which language is founded. But Tillich points to moments of linguistic self-transcendence in which language expresses the union of the person who speaks with that which the person speaks of.[25] Here there is something that transcends the basic subject-object, self-world structure of finite being; one is empowered through the agency of the power of being-itself to transcend the ambiguities of language.

These experiences of empowerment suggest that Tillich's "being-itself" does have a referent. Consider three points. First, in all of these examples of empowerment, being-itself is given to consciousness. The charge that it is nonsensical to speak of being conscious of a reality beyond conceptualization is here overturned by a demonstration that there are phenomena in which ontological poles—of which human beings are unquestionably conscious, according to Tillich—interact in such a manner as to point to a more fundamental reality that transcends them. Such

---

[24]See *ST*, 2:78ff.

[25]See *ST*, 3:253.

phenomena are characterized by a tripartite dialectic in which the first two moments are provided by the structure of being as given to consciousness while the third moment stands outside that structure. One is conscious in such phenomena of being-itself as a special sort of power.[26]

Second, the reality one is conscious of in these phenomena, while it lies beyond the structure of being and thus cannot be positively characterized, is not "empty" in the sense that its presence is consistent with all possible states of affairs. It could not be experienced as a power if that were the case, for its character as power means that it must be contrastable with a state of affairs it transforms. It is experienced as the third part of a dialectic, contrastable with the first two parts. That this power of being is given to consciousness as lying beyond the structure of being in which objects can stand over against other objects, and at the same time as some-

---

[26]At certain points in his writings, Tillich claims that there is such a thing as an "immediate" awareness of being-itself (see especially "The Two Types of Philosophy of Religion," in *Theology of Culture,* ed. Robert C. Kimball [London: Oxford University Press, 1959] 10-29). If this awareness is interpreted as undialectical, that is, independent of the interaction of the poles of the structure of finite being, then one would have no defense to the objection above, as one would if basing awareness upon empowerment. This is the first reason for emphasizing the clearly dialectical awareness of being-itself encountered in the phenomenon of religious empowerment.

A second reason for avoiding a discussion of an undialectical awareness is that some of the points at which Tillich seems to be speaking of an immediate awareness can be interpreted as an awareness of being-itself simply as *demand.* Tillich asserts that one is aware, through the notions of *verum ipsum* and *bonum ipsum* respectively, of an unconditional element in the use of theoretical and practical reason (*ST,* 1:206-208). But it could be argued that one is aware of truth itself and the good itself not directly but as goals, as demanded by reason.

Third, Tillich's system emphasizes the dialectical awareness of being-itself: in chapter 3, where the method of correlation is treated, the phenomenon of empowerment is shown to be central to the whole structure of the hermeneutic provided by the *Systematic Theology.*

Finally, some of Tillich's statements seem to contradict the idea that there is a simple, undialectical awareness of being-itself. Later in this chapter, it will be shown that all awareness of being-itself, according to Tillich, must be mediated through symbols. And in the last section of chapter 2, it will be shown that the truth of a religious symbol is never immediately certain.

how differentiated from the structure, leads Tillich to use metaphorical expressions such as the "depth" of the structure of being and the "ground of being" to describe being-itself.

Third, while the problem involved in thinking the relationship between being-itself and finite being as a causal one has not yet been solved, the three phenomena examined suggest that it is legitimate to call being-itself the source of the transformation of the finite realm.

The phenomenon of empowerment is thus the experiential basis for Tillich's discussion of being-itself. Being-itself is best described, then, according to Tillich himself, with the metaphor "*power* of being."[27] Indeed, a survey shows that the word *power* appears frequently in Tillich's writings, always in connection with his ontology. This connection of power with ontology puts Tillich in good company: "From Plato and Aristotle on, the concept of power plays an important role in ontological thought."[28]

Consider, first, the use of the word *power* in Tillich's analysis of human being. It has been shown that power in one of the forms in which it affects human consciousness is the key to being-itself. Tillich therefore defines the being of man and woman in terms of power. He seems always to have been attracted to the Nietzschean philosophy of life with its emphasis on power and will, and he connects his attraction with his career-long interest in Schelling.[29] However, Tillich recognizes that the human spirit is not constituted by power alone, by mere undirected vitality. Human being also involves the element of meaning.[30] Thus, in Tillich's *Systematic Theology,* his definition of "spirit"—of the human dimension of life—is that it is the "unity of power and meaning."[31] Again, in his essay "The Idea and the Ideal of Personality," he begins, "Personality is that being which

---

[27]See, for example, Tillich, *The Courage to Be,* 179; *Love, Power, and Justice,* 35, 37.

[28]Tillich, *The Courage to Be,* 26.

[29]See Tillich, *Gesammelte Werke,* 1:9.

[30]See Tillich, *The Courage to Be,* 80-84.

[31]*ST,* 3:22.

has power over itself."[32] The ontological character of this claim is shown a few pages later:

> Personality, the possession of control over oneself, is rooted in the structure of being as being. . . . The unconditional character of the demand to become personal is the ethical expression of the ontological structure of being-itself. This is the religious foundation of the idea of personality.[33]

Power is thus central to human being.

The use of the word *power* and its connection with ontology is not limited to Tillich's discussion of human being. He claims that "there is power of being, the power of resisting the threat of nonbeing, for all beings from the atom to the human person."[34] Even social and political power, which interested Tillich throughout his theological development (consider, for example, his 1931 article "Das Problem der Macht" and his 1965 lecture "Shadow and Substance: A Theory of Power")[35] must be seen in the light of ontological analysis. One can therefore speak, at least analogically, of the "power of being" of a social group or of the state.[36]

The formal centrality of empowerment in Tillich's thought, then, is reflected materially in his use of the word *power*. The word is pervasive and is never considered apart from the reality of being-itself, the "power of being" revealed in the phenomenon of empowerment.

---

[32]Paul Tillich, "The Idea and the Ideal of Personality," in *The Protestant Era*, 115.

[33]Ibid., 118.

[34]Paul Tillich, "Shadow and Substance: A Theory of Power," in *Political Expectation*, ed. James Luther Adams (New York: Harper and Row, 1971) 116.

[35]"Das Problem der Macht" is translated by Elsa Talmey as "The Problem of Power," in Tillich, *The Interpretation of History*, 179-202. Regarding "Shadow and Substance," see n. 34 above.

[36]See, for example, Tillich, *The Courage to Be*, 88-89; "The Idea and the Ideal of Personality," 125; "Shadow and Substance," 116-19; *Love, Power, and Justice*, 91-106. Note that this last work gives book-length treatment to the various types of power and their common ontological foundation.

The notion of being-itself is, from the perspective of Tillich's phenomenological ontology, legitimate and fundamental. However, it cannot be positively, nonrelationally described, with accidental predication, essential predication, or identity statements. It is unique. Thus it is that, although one's desire to understand being-itself and to make assertions about it is justifiable, "every assertion about being-itself is either metaphorical or symbolic."[37]

Religion and Being-itself

Tillich defines religion as ultimate concern:

> The religious concern is ultimate; it excludes all other concerns from ultimate significance; it makes them preliminary. The ultimate concern is unconditional, independent of any conditions of character, desire, or circumstance. The unconditional concern is total: no part of ourselves or of our world is excluded from it.[38]

Thus, the first "formal criterion" of Tillich's theology is that "*the object of theology is what concerns us ultimately. Only those propositions are theological which deal with their object in so far as it can become a matter of ultimate concern for us.*"[39] Tillich points out that the word *concern* here has a dual meaning: on the one hand it signifies the act of religious consciousness; on the other it signifies the object of that act of consciousness. Both the subjective element—one's act of concern—and the objective element—that which one is concerned about—must be ultimate if one's religion is to be genuine.[40]

What, then, is the character of the object of ultimate concern? The second "formal criterion" of theology answers: "*Our ultimate concern is that which determines our being or not-being. Only those statements are*

---

[37]Tillich, *The Courage to Be*, 179.

[38]*ST*, 1:11-12.

[39]Ibid., 12.

[40]Paul Tillich, *Dynamics of Faith* (New York: Harper and Row, 1957) 10.

theological which deal with their object in so far as it can become a matter of being or not-being for us."[41] Tillich elaborates on this statement:

> Nothing can be of ultimate concern for us which does not have the power of threatening and saving our being. The term "being" in this context does not designate existence in time and space. Existence is continuously threatened and saved by things and events which have no ultimate concern for us. But the term "being" means the whole of human reality, the structure, the meaning, and the aim of existence. All this is threatened; it can be lost or saved. Man is ultimately concerned about his being and meaning. "To be or not to be" in *this* sense is a matter of ultimate, unconditional, total, and infinite concern.[42]

Thus, there can be only one *proper* object of ultimate concern: "only that which is the ground of our being and meaning should concern us ultimately."[43] Being-itself—that which is revealed to consciousness in the phenomena discussed above—is the legitimate object of religion. What is more, the *way* in which being-itself is revealed—as a source of empowerment—makes it legitimate, for what is of concern here is that which has "the power of threatening and saving our being," "that which determines our being or not-being."[44] For example, recall how courage, as a manifestation of being-itself, negated nonbeing's negation of being.

Not only is the empowering manifestation of being-itself the proper object of religious concern, according to Tillich, that phenomenon is religious by its very nature. First, being-itself is given to consciousness only when one is in a state of ultimate concern.

> That which is ultimate gives itself only to the attitude of ultimate concern. It is the correlate of an unconditional concern but not a "highest thing" called "the absolute" or "the unconditioned," about which we could argue in detached objectivity. It is the object of total surrender, demanding also the surrender of our subjectivity while we look at it. It

---

[41]*ST*, 1:14.

[42]Ibid.

[43]Paul Tillich, *Biblical Religion and the Search for Ultimate Reality* (Chicago: University of Chicago Press, 1955) 51.

[44]*ST*, 1:14.

is a matter of infinite passion and interest (Kierkegaard), making us its
object whenever we try to make it our object.[45]

Tillich goes on to say that ordinary human reason cannot grasp being-itself,[46] thereby verifying the statement that being-itself cannot be conceptualized. Consciousness of being-itself transcends the structure of reason
and can be termed "the depth of reason."[47] According to Tillich, the depth
of reason is precisely what, in traditional theological terms, should be called
"revelation."[48] The revelatory character of the manifestation of being-itself to consciousness is reinforced by the impossibility of coercing consciousness of being-itself. While being-itself is available only through
ultimate concern, every attitude of ultimate concern does not produce a
consciousness of being-itself. The consciousness of being-itself as New
Being (discussed in the second example of empowerment), for instance,
is present, according to Tillich, through the New Testament picture of Jesus as the Christ. The origin of that picture is a historical event, meaning
that "it is *given* in history,"[49] not produced by a desire to intuit being-itself. While philosophy can ask the ontological question and consider the
philosophical implications of the phenomena in which being-itself is manifest, the phenomena themselves are matters of religious experience.

   Tillich declares that everything said about being-itself must be symbolic. If being-itself is central to religion, it follows that "man's ultimate
concern must be expressed symbolically."[50] Furthermore, because Tillich
refers to being-itself in its role as the proper object of ultimate concern as

---

[45]Ibid., 12.

[46]See, for example, ibid., 119.

[47]See ibid., 79-81. Tillich asserts that, in addition to reason as a property of
human being, there is also "objective reason," the *logos* structure of reality that
renders it cognizable by human "subjective reason." If the notion of the "depth
of reason" is taken as the depth that grounds subjective and objective reason, it
must be equivalent to being-itself, for two poles of the structure of finite being
have been transcended.

[48]See ibid., 71-159.

[49]Ibid., 42.

[50]Tillich, *Dynamics of Faith*, 41.

"God," everything said about God must be symbolic. While the latter assertion may seem straightforward at first (we are accustomed to being told that religious discourse employs symbols, if not that all religious discourse is symbolic), a closer look shows it to be plagued with difficulties. Indeed, a large body of secondary literature has arisen that argues that one cannot meaningfully speak of symbolic discourse about God when God is conceived of as Tillich's being-itself. An investigation of this literature will provide a better understanding of Tillich's position.

In a 1940 article, Wilbur Urban warned that there was danger of "pan-symbolism" in Tillich's claim that *everything* said about the divine is symbolic: "the notion of symbolic knowledge (and symbolic truth) is meaningless except in contrast with nonsymbolic knowledge."[51] That is to say, it is meaningless to state that something can be spoken of only in symbolic terms, for if there is no literal knowledge of that thing, one will not know what properties it has and thus will have no knowledge of what the symbolic statements are symbolic expressions of, nor in what sense they are symbolic rather than literal.

Urban's point did not go unnoticed. Tillich himself reports that

> an early criticism by Professor Urban of Yale forced me to acknowledge that in order to speak of symbolic knowledge one must delimit the symbolic realm by an unsymbolic statement. I was grateful for this criticism, and under its impact I became suspicious of any attempts to make the concept of symbol all-embracing and therefore meaningless. The unsymbolic statement which implies the necessity of religious symbolism is that God is being-itself, and as such beyond the subject-object structure of everything that is.[52]

There is, in other words, one nonsymbolic statement that can be made of God.

Does Tillich accomplish anything by saying that the one literal statement that can be made about God is that he is being-itself? If Tillich is to avoid the problem pointed out by Urban, he must also qualify his earlier

---

[51]Wilbur Urban, "Prof. Tillich's Theory of the Religious Symbol," *Journal of Liberal Religion* 2 (Summer 1940): 36.

[52]Paul Tillich, "Reply to Interpretation and Criticism," in *The Theology of Paul Tillich*, 379.

statement that everything said about being-itself must be symbolic; otherwise he falls into pan-symbolism all over again. However, he *can* qualify that statement, because one can make negative and relational propositions about being-itself that are quite literal. It is known, for instance, that being-itself is not a being and that it is the source of courage.

The most accurate understanding of Tillich's position, then, is that all statements about God that are both *positive* and *nonrelational*, other than the one that God is being-itself, must be symbolic. This reformulation, however, accomplishes very little. Several problems result. First, there is the problem of testing the accuracy of such a positive, nonrelational symbol of God as being-itself. William Alston puts the matter this way: "Since we can say nothing nonsymbolically about being-itself, a given symbol cannot be judged in terms of the reality or unreality of that aspect of being-itself which it is being used to symbolize."[53] According to my interpretation of Tillich's position, one would be able to check the adequacy of a symbol intended to communicate a negative or relational fact about being-itself, but Alston's criticism would hold in the case of positive, nonrelational symbols. In fact, one can go further than Alston and say that not only could one not check the accuracy of what such symbols expressed, one could not even know *what* they expressed. If it is true that such symbols cannot be translated into literal terms, then symbols expressing positive, nonrelational facts about being-itself are the sort of "irreducible metaphors" Paul Edwards claims must be deemed unintelligible.[54]

---

[53]William P. Alston, "Tillich's Conception of a Religious Symbol," in *Religious Experience and Truth*, ed. Sidney Hook (New York: New York University Press, 1961) 18; see also his "Tillich on Idolatry," *Journal of Religion* 38 (October 1958): 263-67.

[54]Paul Edwards, "Prof. Tillich's Confusions," *Mind* 74 (April 1965): 199-200. Some commentators have sought to mitigate Edwards's point by suggesting that, while symbolic statements about God cannot, as Tillich understands them, actually be translated into literal terms, such statements can be at least partially clarified. They are not, in other words, totally "irreducible." William Rowe suggests that when Tillich interprets propositions about God—which use religious language—in terms of propositions about being-itself—which use ontological language—although both languages must be symbolic, ontological language is

In other words, the problem connected with pan-symbolism returns to haunt an individual symbol as soon as that symbol is said to be irreducibly symbolic: one cannot know what properties of the thing in question are being symbolically described nor in what sense the description is symbolic rather than literal.[55]

One does not really get to the root of the problem with Tillich's position, however, until one turns from the irreducibility of his symbols to being-itself as the reason for their irreducibility. Critics such as Alston and Edwards are correct in claiming that if no literal translation of a symbol is possible then its accuracy cannot be checked nor its meaning known. Such is the case with any irreducible metaphor or symbol. But note that in the case of a symbol purporting to express a positive, nonrelational fact about being-itself, it is not simply that the symbol *in fact* tells nothing. Rather, the symbol cannot *in principle* tell anything because of the nature of its object, for being-itself does not possess positive, nonrelational attributes: it makes no more sense to speak of a symbolic description of nonexistent properties than it does to speak of a literal description. Thus, Lewis Ford's assertion is correct that

> it is Tillich's ontology that prevents his religious symbols from doing the job they were fashioned for. . . . All positive content of the symbols is canceled out by the clear negative directive that they must refer to that

---

somehow less symbolic and more nearly conceptual than religious language. See William Rowe, *Religious Symbols and God: A Philosophical Study of Tillich's Theology* (Chicago: University of Chicago Press, 1968) 183-94. Compare Robert P. Scharlemann's suggestion that Tillich can avoid the problem of irreducibility by using a strategy other than translation, namely, by correlating religious and ontological language, in *Reflection and Doubt in the Thought of Paul Tillich* (New Haven: Yale University Press, 1969) 88-89.

[55]What "irreducible" means here is that no literal translation can be given. "Irreducible" does not mean simply that a particular symbol or metaphor cannot be translated into literal terms *without remainder*, for no effective metaphors or symbols can simply be replaced by a literal formulation. A metaphor found in a good poem, for example, describes something that can also be described in literal terms, but the two descriptions are undertaken in different ways and with different effects upon the reader.

which is not a being, and we are given no clear guidelines as to what their remaining positive content could possibly be.[56]

According to the objections raised by Urban, Alston, Edwards, and Ford,[57] Tillich's position is a weak one. On the one hand, one can make literal negative or relational assertions about God as being-itself. And one can supply roughly equivalent literal assertions for symbols of God intended to express negative or relational facts. But, on the other hand, one can no more make positive, nonrelational symbolic assertions about God than one can make positive, nonrelational literal assertions. God as being-itself is beyond the self-world structure of being and does not possess certain characteristics and lack others.

Tillich's dilemma might be compared to the situation Thomas Aquinas faced in discussing language about God. Thomas wanted to find a way to speak about God using assertions that were not merely negative or relational.[58] His solution, of course, was analogical predication. Now Tillich often suggests that when he says that one must speak symbolically about

---

[56]Lewis Ford, "Tillich's One Nonsymbolic Statement: A propos of a Recent Study by Rowe," *Journal of the American Academy of Religion* 38 (June 1970): 176-77.

[57]The sorts of complaints raised by Urban, Alston, Edwards, and Ford about the untenability of Tillich's assertion that religious symbols are descriptive of being-itself have been discussed by numerous other scholars as well. See Walter Kaufmann, "Symbols: Contra Tillich," in *Critique of Religion and Philosophy* (New York: Harper and Row, 1958; Princeton Paperback, 1978) 189-96; William L. Reese, "Analogy, Symbolism, and Linguistic Analysis," *Review of Metaphysics* 13 (March 1960): 447-68; Sidney Hook, "The Atheism of Paul Tillich," in *Religious Experience and Truth*, 59-64; Vincent Thomas, "Darkness or Light?" in *Religious Experience and Truth*, 76-82; Bowman L. Clarke, "God and the Symbolic in Tillich," *Anglican Theological Review* 43 (July 1961): 302-11; William A. Johnson, "Tillich's Religious Symbol," *Encounter* 23 (Summer 1962): 325-42; H. D. McDonald, "The Symbolic Theology of Paul Tillich," *Scottish Journal of Theology* 17 (December 1964): 414-30; R. F. Aldwinckle, "Tillich's Theory of Religious Symbolism," *Canadian Journal of Theology* 10 (April 1964): 110-17; John Y. Fenton, "Being-itself and Religious Symbolism," *Journal of Religion* 45 (April 1965): 73-86.

[58]See St. Thomas Aquinas, *Summa Theologiae*, vol. 1, pt. 1, Q.13, a.2.

God he has analogical predication in mind.[59] But the notion of analogy formulated by Thomas, whether or not it provides a legitimate positive, nonrelational description of God as he conceived of him, is not an option for Tillich. The Thomistic form of analogical predication is based upon the Thomistic doctrine of *analogia entis*. One facet of that doctrine is the claim that God, though he transcends the finite world, is still a being, and that it therefore makes sense to predicate certain qualities of him. In contrast, Tillich, by claiming that God as being-itself is not a being, runs into difficulties. Again, it is nonsensical to attempt to predicate qualities of Tillich's God, whether with literal or analogical language. Tillich remains limited to negative and relational propositions. Indeed, Tillich himself at one point suggests, in response to a Catholic commentator, that his use of analogy is basically negative: "I believe you are right when you say that my understanding of *analogia* is more negative-protesting than positive-affirming. I am more worried about the idolic character of traditional theology and popular beliefs about God than you are."[60]

The crucial differences between Thomas and Tillich is another important subject of the secondary literature on Tillich. Ford, for example, emphasizes the point that analogical predication presupposes that God is a being. Thomas, he reminds his readers, understood *all* being as analogous. This perception allowed him to specify a difference between finite being and God—they are not exactly the same but, rather, analogous—without portraying it as a radical discontinuity between the finite world and God—an analogous relationship holds among all levels of being, including those contained within the finite world. In contrast, Tillich posits a radical discontinuity between beings and God as being-itself such that God is not a being at all.[61] Hence it is impossible to predicate anything of him, analogically or otherwise.

---

[59]See, for example, *ST*, 1:131, 239-40.

[60]Tillich's reply to Gustave Weigel, "The Theological Significance of Paul Tillich," in *Paul Tillich in Catholic Thought*, rev. ed., ed. Thomas F. O'Meara and Donald M. Weisser (New York: Image Books, 1969) 55.

[61]See Lewis Ford, "Tillich and Thomas: The Analogy of Being," *Journal of Religion* 46 (April 1966): 229-45.

Jean Richard augments this discussion by noting that when Tillich speaks of the *analogia entis* existing between beings and being-itself, he means only that all beings depend upon being-itself as the power of being that allows them to be at all; the *analogia entis* refers to the participation of beings in the *dynamic* of being-itself rather than in the *form* of being-itself.[62]

The sort of predication involved in Thomas's use of analogy has led some commentators to conclude that there is even confusion in using the words *analogy* and *symbol* as synonyms. "Symbol" suggests nonliteral expression, which seems to be how Tillich intends the word to be understood. "Analogy," in contrast, at least as Thomas employs it, is not really nonliteral. Josef Schmitz points out that for Thomas, only the way in which human beings understand and express a particular perfection—when applied to God—is nonliteral, because human understanding and expression is borrowed from human knowledge of and speech about finite beings. The perfection itself, on the other hand, belongs literally to God.[63] Thus, the position embraced by Thomas is, to borrow Gustave Weigel's apt words, neither univocal literalism nor unliteral symbolism but analogous literalism.[64]

These arguments lead many who are sympathetic to Thomas's position to conclude that, while Thomas's analogical predication is objectively rooted in the nature of reality, Tillich's symbols are merely subjective. Tillich's symbols can provide no positive, nonrelational information about the being of God; hence, they simply express subjective impressions of God. George McClean, for example, advocates this view.[65]

---

[62]Jean Richard, "Symbolisme et analogie selon Paul Tillich," *Laval theologique et philosophique* 33 (1977): 199.

[63]See Josef Schmitz, *Die apologetische Theologie Paul Tillichs* (Mainz: Matthias-Grünwald, 1966) 101-104. The relevant passage in Thomas is found in *Summa Theologiae*, vol. 1, pt. 1, Q.13, a.3.

[64]Gustave Weigel, "Myth, Symbol, and Analogy," in *Paul Tillich in Catholic Thought*, 253.

[65]See George McClean, "Symbol and Analogy: Tillich and Thomas," in *Paul Tillich in Catholic Thought*, 195-240. Tillich has been charged with subjectivism by more than those who compare him to Thomas. Compare Helmut Gollwitzer, *The Existence of God as Confessed by Faith*, trans. James W. Leitch (London: SCM, 1965) 164-70.

This comparison of Tillich with Thomas[66] seems, then, only to confirm that Tillich can make only negative or relational statements about his God. Symbols cannot extend this field of information. Thus, it appears that the only legitimate use of symbols for a Tillichian, beyond expressing the subjective states of the believer, would be to express figuratively negative and relational facts, which can all be expressed literally. Perhaps figurative expression has a certain value for religious piety, communicating the facts more powerfully and making their existential relevance clear.[67]

Tillich's critics seem to share the assumption that the role of a symbol, religious or otherwise, is to communicate information, to provide facts. What distinguishes a symbol from a literal statement, in this view, is that a symbol communicates figuratively. Analogical predication differs somewhat in that it is partly literal, but it too is seen as communicating information. Tillich's use of symbols in relation to God as being-itself therefore must fail because there is no positive and nonrelational information to be had about being-itself.

But scrutiny of the scope of Tillich's position reveals a deeper connection between religious consciousness and symbols than the desire to communicate information about God as the object of ultimate concern: Tillich indicates that there is not even consciousness of being-itself as the proper object of ultimate concern without symbols.

I have already noted the duality in ultimate concern constituted by the distinction between concern as the act of consciousness and the object

---

[66]For like comparisons, see Edward O'Connor, "Paul Tillich: An Impression," in *Paul Tillich in Catholic Thought*, 56-75; Christoph Rhein, *Paul Tillich: Philosoph und Theologe* (Stuttgart: Evangelisches Verlagswerk, 1957) 170-79; A. J. Zabala, "Myth and Symbol: An Analysis of Myth and Symbol in Paul Tillich," Ph.D. diss., Institut Catholique de Paris, 1959, 301-308; Battista Mondin, *The Principle of Analogy in Protestant and Catholic Theology* (The Hague: Martinus Nijhoff, 1963) 118-46, 174-76; Klaus-Dieter Nörenberg, *Analogia Imaginis: Der Symbolbegriff in der Theologie Paul Tillichs* (Gütersloh: Gütersloher Verlagshaus Gerd Mohn, 1966) 166-73; Michael Simpson, "Paul Tillich: Symbolism and Objectivity," *Heythrop Journal* 8 (June 1967): 293-309; Matthias von Kriegstein, *Paul Tillichs Methode der Korrelation und Symbolbegriff* (Hildesheim: Gerstenberg, 1975) 134-38.

[67]Compare Lewis Ford, "The Three Strands of Tillich's Theory of Religious Symbols," *Journal of Religion* 46 (January 1966): 104-30.

of consciousness. Also inherent in it is another duality: a tension between its concrete element and its ultimate element. On the one hand, the proper object of ultimate concern is being-itself, a reality beyond the self-world structure and hence not an object that can be set over against the self as subject. On the other hand, "it is impossible to be concerned about something which cannot be encountered concretely,"[68] for the object of concern must be such that "we can encounter it, be grasped by it, know it, and act toward it."[69] If being-itself is to be given to consciousness, it must be able somehow to become an object of consciousness, to become a "logical object" even if it is in no way an "ontological object."[70]

Tillich explains his notion of concreteness: "Something that is merely particular has a limited concreteness because it must exclude other particular realities in order to maintain itself as concrete. Only that which has the power of representing everything particular is absolutely concrete."[71] The most concrete of all entities is therefore a personal life,[72] for it is a single, unified entity containing not only self-consciousness, but all the preconscious dimensions of being as well. A personal life thus has great representative power.

To say that ultimate concern requires a concrete element so that being-itself can become an object of consciousness is to say that ultimate concern requires symbols. Being-itself is not itself a concrete entity, so something concrete must stand in for it, must serve as a symbol for it. The symbol is the aperture within the structure of being through which being-itself can be intuited. This role of symbol as concrete content of an ultimate concern is different from its purported role as information provider.[73] Using Til-

-----

[68]*ST*, 1:211.

[69]Ibid., 21.

[70]Ibid., 171-74.

[71]Ibid., 16.

[72]Ibid., 150.

[73]Compare Guyton Hammond's observation regarding Tillich's use of sym-

lich's own term, one may designate the former function "representation."

Hans-Georg Gadamer's view of the symbol's role as "pure representation" (*reine Vertreten*)[74] concurs with the above designation: "Symbols do not need to be pictorial. They perform their representative function through their mere existence and manifesting of themselves, but of themselves they say nothing about what they symbolize."[75] Tillich's claim that religious symbols "are not true or false in the sense of cognitive judgments" supports his belief that religious symbols represent being-itself by standing in for it rather than by providing information about it.[76] Such symbols "provide no objective knowledge, but yet a true awareness."[77] By serving as the concrete content of an ultimate concern, a symbol stands in for being-itself, thereby providing an awareness of being-itself different from a grasp of certain facts about being-itself. There is a "symbolic consciousness" of being-itself.

---

bols: "there are important differences between a symbol used in an effort to conceptualize the Divine and a symbol which functions as a mediator of the divine Presence." *The Power of Self-Transcendence: An Introduction to the Philosophical Theology of Paul Tillich* (St. Louis: Bethany Press, 1966) 120-21.

[74]Hans-Georg Gadamer, *Truth and Method*, translation ed. Garrett Barden and John Cumming (New York: Continuum, 1975) 134; *Wahrheit und Methode*, 4th ed. (Tübingen: J. C. B. Mohr, 1975) 144.

[75]Gadamer, *Truth and Method*, 136. Gadamer actually goes farther here than one needs to go or can go in a Tillichian context. He proceeds to say that "signs and symbols alike do not—like the picture—acquire their functional significance from their own content, but must be taken as signs or symbols. We call this origin of their functional significance their 'institution' " (p. 137). Tillich does not allow that symbols are arbitrary in this sense and can be intentionally created. While religious symbols, for Tillich, do not provide direct information about being-itself, they do have an "original affinity" with being-itself. See chapter 2 below.

[76]Paul Tillich, "Existential Analysis and Religious Symbols," in *Contemporary Problems in Religion*, ed. Harold A. Basilius (Detroit: Wayne University Press, 1956) 54.

[77]Paul Tillich, "The Religious Symbol," in *Religious Experience and Truth*, 316.

Symbols are thus, in an important sense, the source of a fundamental empowerment in which being-itself transforms the structure of finite being. The line of reasoning leading to this statement can be shown, using courage as an example:

1. Being-itself is the source of courage.
2. But being-itself can be given to consciousness only in an attitude of ultimate concern.
3. The object of ultimate concern must be concrete, although the proper object of ultimate concern is being-itself.
4. Thus, being-itself is given to consciousness only through a concrete entity that stands in for being-itself, a symbol.
5. It follows that courage is available only through the medium of symbols.

Certain religious symbols must be deemed empowering symbols.

How is being-itself given to consciousness in a phenomenon such as courage? I have argued that the dialectic of empowerment, when it involves fundamental poles of the structure of being, answers the objection that one cannot meaningfully speak of a consciousness of that which is beyond differentiation. But suppose that the author of that original objection replies: "True, the dialectic of courage establishes the legitimacy of the ontological question and the notion of being-itself, for it clearly points beyond the structure of being. But that is all that it does. It points beyond the structure but does not actually present being-itself to consciousness, for all one is conscious of is the transformation within the structure of finitude. One is conscious of the effect of the power of being upon the structure, not of the power of being *itself;* one simply concludes that being-itself must be the source of the experience."

The discovery that a symbol is the indirect source of courage allows one to answer this new objection. In the dialectic of courage, one is conscious, first, of nonbeing's conflict with being. This consciousness is given through the mood of anxiety. One is then conscious of the change wrought by the appearance of courage. In addition, however, one is conscious of the religious symbol, not only as *concrete symbol,* but also as *at this moment providing courage.* Thus, through the medium of the symbol one is made conscious not only of the objective results of the manifestation of the power of being within the structure of being but of the power of being itself as it creates those results.

The status of the symbol as the source of empowerment helps solve another problem: how can one speak of being-itself empowering something without employing the category of causality, which, since it is a category of finite being and thinking, ought to be employed only within the finite sphere? Taking courage again as an example: the proximate source of courage is a symbol, the symbol "God" for instance. Now this symbol is a finite entity lying within the structure of finitude. It can be said, then, that the *symbol* does indeed stand in a causal relationship to the courage it empowers.[78] And because the symbol here represents being-itself, being-itself indirectly is a *cause* of courage. The power of being is refracted into the finite world through the prism of the religious symbol.

The discovery that religious empowerment is mediated by symbols is important not only for one's understanding of empowerment but also for one's grasp of the role of symbol. Over against the secondary literature's critique of Tillich's doctrine of symbolism, I have set the claim that the primary function of the religious symbol is not to provide information about being-itself but to stand in for it, to represent it. But suppose a critic such as Alston were to reply that even with regard to symbols as representations, his analysis of Tillich's position—that "since we can say nothing about being-itself, a given symbol cannot be judged in terms of the reality or unreality of that aspect of being-itself which it is being used to symbolize"—still holds. Can one determine, Alston might ask, that a particular symbol represents being-itself? There is not, after all, any positive and nonrelational knowledge of being-itself that could be juxtaposed with the symbol in question.

One can respond that a genuine symbol of being-itself empowers a phenomenon such as courage. It has been shown that such a phenomenon can be said to make being-itself present to consciousness. If a given symbol

---

[78]Tillich does allow that causality applies within the realm of human consciousness: "The causal scheme must not be identified with a deterministic scheme. Causality is removed neither by the indeterminacy of subatomic processes nor by the creative character of biological and psychological processes. Nothing in these realms occurs without a preceding situation or constellation which is its cause. Nothing has the power of depending on itself without a causal nexus; nothing is 'absolute.'" *ST*, 1:196.

provides religious empowerment, it surely can be said to represent being-itself.

Tillich's system implies that symbols play several roles in religion. First, there is the minor role of providing negative or relational data about being-itself in figurative form. While this is not a primary function of symbols, its use can be found in Tillich's work.[79] The symbol's second and fundamental role is that of "representation." On the basis of my investigation in this chapter, the representative role can be divided into four sub-roles.

First, the representative symbol provides a concrete object for consciousness, one that, in the case of genuine ultimate concern, contains characteristics directing consciousness toward its own limits, toward its unconditional depth. The notion of a Supreme Being, for example, can function in this fashion, for it directs thought beyond the realm of the finite. The idea of a Supreme Being therefore has certain "affinities" with being-itself, even though a Supreme Being would in literal terms be one being among others. Here, there is already a limited awareness, a symbolic consciousness, of being-itself as the negation of the negation of being, for when consciousness is directed toward its depth, it looks beyond the structure of finitude in which nonbeing negates being.

Once consciousness has been directed beyond the negation of being by nonbeing, the phenomenon of empowerment can be experienced: acting as the source of this empowerment is the second sub-role of the representative symbol. In other words, having first served as an object directing thought beyond the negation of being occurring within finitude, the symbol can then serve as the source of the negation of the negation of being in the more potent sense of causing a self to overcome the threat of nonbeing. For once one is made aware of a dimension of reality beyond the region in which nonbeing negates being, one is free to understand oneself as grounded in that other dimension and thereby free to live courageously, to overcome existential distortion, and at least partially to transcend ambiguity.

---

[79]Tillich himself does not sort out the different uses of symbol as clearly as one might wish. This lack of distinction leads to inconsistency in his system. See chapter 3 below.

This movement from the representative symbol's first sub-role to its second suggests that being-itself is not a power existing in and of itself apart from human consciousness, a mysterious force human beings tap into in order to be empowered. Instead, empowerment arises as a result of how one conceives of one's being. One experiences empowerment when one understands oneself as grounded in a dimension of reality beyond the finite structure of being.

But the movement from the representative symbol's first sub-role to its second also suggests that being-itself is not simply reducible to the experience of empowerment. While being-itself qua transforming power first appears in the experience of empowerment, there is still a sense in which being-itself, as mediated to consciousness through the symbol, is the *source* of empowerment. Empowerment as the actual negation of the negation of being does not arise within consciousness spontaneously but only as a result of one's having a symbolic consciousness of being-itself as the depth of the self-world structure of being. The symbol must first direct consciousness beyond the finite structure of being if empowerment is to occur.

If the representative symbol's first sub-role is directing consciousness beyond the structure of finitude, and the second is acting as the proximate source of empowerment, the third is its enabling one to be conscious of that power. The symbol makes it possible, as noted above, to be conscious not only of the results of the manifestation of the power of being within the structure of finitude but also of the power itself.

Once the representative symbol has provided this threefold service, the person for whom it has so functioned no doubt will subsequently use it to refer to the experience of being-itself that it has made possible. In other words, the symbol will be used to denote this experience and to communicate about it to others. This fourth sub-role of the representative symbol has nothing to do with providing information about being-itself. It serves, rather, as a means for referring to the experience that the symbol has previously made possible.

In this first chapter, I have investigated how Tillich's thinking about symbols arises out of his larger ontology and theology. In the following chapter, I shall turn from this connection and concentrate instead upon some of the specific characteristics Tillich attributes to religious symbols. I shall, of course, ask how these characteristics can be fitted into the pattern that has been discerned up to this point.

2

The Nature of Symbols

Chapter 1 dealt with the origin and basic tenets of Tillich's theory of religious symbols; the specific nature of symbols—as Tillich perceives them—can now be detailed. Tillich lists five characteristics as definitive of not just religious symbols but of all genuinely "representative symbols."[1] A "representative symbol" (1) points beyond itself, (2) participates in the reality it represents, (3) cannot be created at will, (4) opens up dimensions of reality that correlate with dimensions of the human spirit, and

---

[1]Paul Tillich, "The Meaning and Justification of Religious Symbols," in *Religious Experience and Truth*, 3. Tillich wishes to distinguish symbols from signs. But some things that he would call signs, such as mathematical figures, are commonly called symbols. Thus he expresses his agreement with the suggestion that symbols that are genuinely symbolic be termed "representative symbols," thereby distinguishing them from those mere signs commonly referred to as symbols. There are, he says, four realms in which representative symbols appear: language, history, the arts, and religion.

(5) possesses integrating and disintegrating power.[2] Answering the question of what constitutes a representative symbol leads to another question: is there a test that will establish whether a particular religious symbol provides a true awareness of being-itself?

The Pointing Quality of Symbols

Symbols and signs, according to Tillich, have one characteristic in common: they both point beyond themselves.[3] That is, something that serves as a sign or a symbol has a function other than to be what it is in and of itself: it must also draw one's attention to something outside itself. This "figurative" quality[4] of signs and symbols is evident, for example, in writing. A word is more than a physical mark on a page: it carries a sense and has a referent. Its sense is what it gives to thought. Its referent is the actual object or reality that the mark on the page is about.[5] But something less obviously figurative may function in the same manner. Suppose that a person tells one how to get through the woods by saying, "When you get

---

[2]The list of characteristics used here is found in Tillich's essay "The Meaning and Justification of Religious Symbols" (pp. 3-11), written in 1960 (hence, relatively late). Other of his articles on symbols contain similar lists, usually with only minor variations. See "The Nature of Religious Language," in *Theology of Culture,* 53-67; "Theology and Symbolism," in *Religious Symbolism,* ed. F. Ernest Johnson (New York: Harper, 1953) 107-16; chapter 4 of *Dynamics of Faith.*

[3]Tillich, *Dynamics of Faith,* 41.

[4]Paul Tillich, "The Word of God," in *Language: An Inquiry into its Meaning and Function,* ed. Ruth Nanda Anshen (New York: Harper, 1957) 132.

[5]This familiar use of the concepts of sense and reference, which Tillich himself does not employ, is derived from Frege's "On Sense and Reference" (also translated as "On Sense and Meaning"), though it abstracts from some of the more technical aspects of Frege's own understanding of the terms. Note, for example, his statement that the sense of a sign is that in which the "mode of presentation" of its object is contained. "On Sense and Meaning," trans. Max Black, in *Translations from the Philosophical Writings of Gottlob Frege,* 3d ed., ed. Peter Geach and Max Black (Totowa NJ: Rowman and Littlefield, 1980) 57.

to the fork in the road, follow the path marked by the large rock." In this instance, a rock has become a sign. It carries a sense—that a certain path is the correct path—and it has a referent—the actual physical path.

Participation
as a Three-Part Whole

If signs and symbols are alike in that they both point beyond themselves, they can also be distinguished. Unlike signs, symbols "participate" in the reality to which they point.[6] What exactly Tillich means by "participation" here has been much disputed, and his use of the term has been greatly criticized.[7] Much of the ambiguity lies in Tillich's use of the word in dangerously varied ways:

> The concept of participation has many functions. A symbol participates in the reality it symbolizes; the knower participates in the known; the lover participates in the beloved; the existent participates in the essences which make it what it is, under the conditions of existence; the individual participates in the destiny of separation and guilt; the Christian participates in the New Being as it is manifest in Jesus as the Christ.[8]

But how exactly does "participation" apply to symbols? I wish to suggest that in order to understand Tillich's statement that the symbol participates in the reality it points to, one must see participation as the third part of a three-part whole comprised of: *original affinity, representation,* and *participation.*

Original Affinity

A reality becomes a candidate to symbolize another reality through *original affinity:* the first reality in some way naturally calls to mind the

---

[6]*ST,* 1:239.

[7]See, for example, Lewis Ford, "The Three Strands of Tillich's Theory of Religious Symbols," 104-30, especially 117-24.

[8]*ST,* 1:177.

second. This situation might occur, for example, because the first reality shares certain properties with the second, or because the first reality has some qualities in one sense that the second reality has in another, as when the physical solidity of a stone suggests itself as a symbol for the solidity of a particular person's character. In contrasting symbols and signs, Tillich claims:

> Symbols are nearer to the reality expressed in them. Their direct, immediate, non-symbolic nature must have an original affinity to the symbolic content they represent. If water is used in religious rites, not the power of water as such has the religious effect; but the ritual context in which it stands. But it stands in this context, because it has natural qualities through which it is adequate to its ritual use (purification, regeneration, death and birth, etc.). If the word God, conveying the idea of the highest being, is used for the expression of our unconditional concern, the notions implied in the idea of a highest being make it adequate to stand for the ground and abyss of all being.[9]

This original affinity between symbol and symbolized suggests that a symbol is not chosen arbitrarily as a sign is chosen.[10]

Representation

The original affinity between symbol and symbolized results in the *representative* character of symbols. If a symbol possesses characteristics that give it an original affinity with its referent, it can do more than point to the referent: it can stand in for or represent it[11] just as an ambassador represents a nation.[12] This is the type of representation, of course, discussed in chapter 1 as the primary function of a religious symbol.

----

[9]Paul Tillich, "Symbol and Knowledge: A Response," *Journal of Liberal Religion* 2 (Spring 1941): 204. Compare Paul Tillich, "Water," in James Luther Adams, *Paul Tillich's Philosophy of Culture, Science and Religion* (New York: Harper and Row, 1965) 62-64.

[10]See *ST*, 1:239.

[11]See Tillich, "The Nature of Religious Language," 56. Compare Nörenberg, *Analogia Imaginis*, 135-39.

[12]See Paul Tillich, "Rejoinder," *Journal of Religion* 46 (January 1966): 188.

This representative function is further explained by Tillich's contention that "a symbolic expression is one whose proper meaning is negated by that to which it points. And yet it is also affirmed by it, and this affirmation gives the symbolic expression an adequate basis for pointing beyond itself."[13] In other words, a symbol's qualities—or the sense of a symbolic statement—are both affirmed and denied, affirmed because they do have some affinity with the symbolized and thus can point towards it, denied because they do not literally reflect the symbolized.

This "dialectic of affirmation and negation"[14] converges with what has been said here about representation. The representative *is* in some senses the thing represented. One might say, for example, that a lawyer who represents his or her client before the court is, in a functional sense, that client. This statement exemplifies the affirmative moment. But there is just as obviously a sense in which the representative is *not* the thing represented, hence the negative moment. One might say that representation as a whole is the synthetic moment in the dialectic of affirmation and negation: the concrete unity of a lawyer's being the client and not being the client is representation; the lawyer as the one who both is and is not the client is the one who *stands in for* the client.

Participation

This discussion leads to the third element: participation. Tillich speaks of the relationship between symbol and symbolized as one of *participation,* saying:

> The concept of representation itself implies this relation. The representative of a person or an institution participates in the honor of those whom he is asked to represent; but it is not *he* who is honored, it is that which or he whom he represents. In this sense we can state generally that the symbol participates in the reality of what it symbolizes. It radiates the power of being and meaning of that for which it stands.[15]

[13]*ST*, 1:239.

[14]The phrase is Lewis Ford's. See "The Three Strands of Tillich's Theory of Religious Symbols," 106-13.

[15]Tillich, "The Meaning and Justification of Religious Symbols," 4.

Because the symbol *represents* that which it symbolizes, it is charged with the power and meaning of the symbolized in that the attitude the symbolized produces is also produced by the symbol. Hans-Georg Gadamer's discussion of symbolic representation concurs with this statement:

> A symbol not only points to something, but it represents, in that it takes the place of something. But to take the place of something means to make something present that is not present. . . . Only because the symbol presents in this way the presence of what it represents, is it treated with the reverence due to that which it symbolizes. Such symbols as a crucifix, a flag, a uniform are so representative of what is revered that the latter is present in them.[16]

The examples Tillich uses to express the nature of symbolic participation are similar: "The flag participates in the power and dignity of the nation for which it stands. . . . An attack on the flag is felt as an attack on the majesty of the group in which it is acknowledged. Such an attack is considered blasphemy."[17] Participation, then, as it applies to symbols, refers to the qualities the symbol is experienced as possessing as a representative of the symbolized.[18]

---

[16]Gadamer, *Truth and Method*, 136.

[17]Tillich, *Dynamics of Faith*, 20.

[18]While this view—representation flows from original affinity and participation from representation—does seem to provide a coherent conception of symbolic participation, there are difficulties in how Tillich himself uses the term *participation*. Note that Ford more or less identifies participation with what has been called here original affinity (thus making participation a precondition for representation rather than its result): "Symbolic participation means nothing more than that the symbol bears associative overtones which the sign does not possess and that it possibly bears natural resemblances with that which is symbolized" ("The Three Strands of Tillich's Theory of Religious Symbols," 124). But this definition ignores the different directions involved in original affinity and participation. In the case of the affinity that makes something a candidate to symbolize something else, the movement is from the symbol to the symbolized: the nature of the symbol leads one to think of the symbolized. But in the case of what Tillich calls symbolic participation—at least, in the case of his examples if not in his the-

Representation and Affinity
as Applied to Religious Symbols

It might appear difficult to apply this account of representation and affinity to *religious* symbols—symbols of being-itself—for affinity seems to suggest that there is information about the thing symbolized, that the

---

oretical descriptions—the direction is just the opposite: the honor accruing to the symbolized is transferred to the symbol. Affinity is a precondition for representation, participation a result of representation.

There is some confusion here because in the case of *religious* symbols, Tillich does speak of a kind of participation that precedes representation rather than follows it. The reason that anything at all can become a symbol for that symbolized in religion—being-itself—is that all things have an affinity with being-itself: everything that is "participates in being-itself" (*ST*, 1:239). This sort of participation—call it "general participation"—is to be distinguished from the sort of participation discussed above—call it "symbolic participation"—even though Tillich himself seems often to conflate the two.

First, two different directions can again be distinguished here. General participation means that any reality can serve to direct attention to being-itself; it is a type of original affinity. But there is also that kind of participation, even where religious symbols are concerned, in which there is a movement from symbolized to symbol: one reacts to the eucharistic elements or to the crucifix with reverence and awe, not because of qualities they possess (including the qualities that allow affinity) but because they are imbued with the power and meaning of their referent. General participation is a precondition for religious representation; symbolic participation is a result.

That the two types of participation must be distinguished is made clear, second, by Tillich's application of participation to nonreligious symbols. The flag, for example, participates in the meaning and power of the nation it represents. But this participation is not the same as general participation; the flag does participate in being-itself, but such participation gives it an affinity with the object of religious symbolism, not with the nation. Symbolic participation must therefore be something different from general participation.

The designations "general participation" and "symbolic participation" reflect Nörenberg's *Analogia Imaginis,* where it is argued, though for somewhat different reasons from those provided here, that such a distinction must be made. See pp. 161-65: "Symbolpartizipation und allgemeine Seinspartizipation bei Tillich."

referent can be conceptualized because its characteristics are known. It is true that, in the case of symbolic representation, original affinity is necessary to representation, and that affinity may in fact depend on information provided by the symbol. For example, a rock may have an affinity with Peter because the solidity of the rock suggests the solidity of Peter's character. The material in the symbol that allows for affinity does in this case provide information about the symbolized. But it is easy to find characteristics of finite realities that could be the basis for an affinity with being-itself, even though these characteristics do not provide nonrelational positive information about being-itself.

Recall, first, the legitimacy of the *via negativa*, of making negative statements about being-itself. It is true to say, for instance, that being-itself lies beyond the four categories of finite being and thinking; this statement thus explains the affinity the concept of a god, as expressed in classical mythology, has with being-itself.

> Not only do the images of the gods bear all the characteristics of finitude—this makes them images and gives them concreteness—but they also have characteristics in which categorical finitude is radically transcended. Their identity as finite substances is negated by all kinds of substantial transmutations and expansions, in spite of the sameness of their names. Their temporal limitations are overcome; they are called "immortals" in spite of the fact that their appearance and disappearance are presupposed. Their spatial definiteness is negated when they act as multi- or omni-present, yet they have a special dwelling place with which they are intimately connected. Their subordination to the chain of causes and effects is denied, for overwhelming or absolute power is attributed to them in spite of their dependence on other divine powers and on the influence finite beings have on them.[19]

Thus, the images of the gods have an affinity—admittedly, one lying within the realm of the *via negativa*—with being-itself in that they are said to transgress the boundaries of substance, time, space, and causality. The same can be said for the God of traditional monotheism. That concept of God cannot, for Tillich, be a literal description of being-itself, for such a God, even if the supreme being, is still one being among others and hence

---

[19]*ST*, 1:212-13.

subject to the structures of finitude.[20] But there are aspects of the concept of a supreme being that make it suitable as a symbol, as a representation, of being-itself. Tillich makes a statement to this effect (quoted above with regard to original affinity): "If the word God, conveying the idea of the highest being, is used for the expression of our unconditional concern, the notions implied in the idea of a highest being make it adequate to stand for the ground and abyss of all being."[21] As a highest being, it lies beyond the realm in which all other beings reside.

In addition to the *via negativa*, there is a second approach to discovering affinities with being-itself. Certain realities may suggest being-itself because they have affinities with that which is effected by being-itself within the structure of finite being. In the quest for being-itself, one seeks, for instance, the power to overcome the disrelation between the polar elements of freedom and destiny. Perhaps, then, the notion of healing could be used to symbolize being-itself, for the process of physical healing can be said to have affinities with that empowerment sought from being-itself. In this second approach, the relational properties of being-itself are being used.

A third basis for discovering affinities with being-itself is that everything that exists, according to Tillich, is grounded in being-itself.[22] Thus, everything possesses an affinity with being-itself that makes it a candidate to symbolize that reality. Indeed, Tillich sometimes seems to suggest that this means that no entity or idea is better suited than another to symbolize being-itself, that the affinities discussed thus far serve only to better enable things to symbolize *a particular perspective upon* being-itself.[23] Whatever may be the case, Tillich's writings do establish bases for claiming that religious symbols, too, have affinities with that which they symbolize and that the character of these affinities upholds the rule that only negative, relational knowledge of being-itself is available.

---

[20]See Tillich, *The Courage to Be,* 184-85.

[21]Tillich, "Symbol and Knowledge," 204.

[22]The use of "participates" as in "Everything *participates* in being-itself," has been avoided, since participation in that sense might be confused with the symbolic participation that is part of the affinity-representation-participation complex. See note 18 above.

[23]See *ST,* 1:118.

Hence, religious symbols symbolize being-itself without providing any positive, nonrelational information about being-itself. This accomplishment is explained by the concept of representation. Representation is based upon a symbol's original affinities with its referent, which religious symbols possess either (1) because they suggest truths about being-itself by expressing what it is not, (2) because they suggest what being-itself effects within the structure of finite being, or (3) because they are grounded, like all other things, in being-itself.

Participation
as Applied to Religious Symbols

If from original affinity there results the possibility of representation, from representation there flows participation. How does participation, the third component in the affinity-representation-participation complex, specifically relate to religious symbols? It has been shown that symbolic participation entails that a symbol is perceived as possessing the significance of its referent so that one responds to the symbol as one would respond to the referent. Thus, if a nation's flag is desecrated, the citizens of that nation may be outraged. But surely the flag only indirectly participates in the actual power of the nation: one treats the flag with the respect due the nation, but it would be silly to claim that it literally possessed the military power of the nation, that it could, say, destroy a city by unleashing a nuclear explosion.[24]

Similarly, consider the biblical symbol of the potter and the pot, which represents the God of traditional theism. That symbol expresses, among other things, the causal power God is thought to exercise. Now it may be that when one reflects on this symbol one is awed by the omnipotence of God. In that sense the symbol must be said to participate in the reality to which it points. But clearly, the symbol itself does not possess the causal power it represents: it cannot, for example, bring new worlds into being. The symbol and its power are matters of human consciousness and operate within that realm, while the causal power symbolized belongs to a being separate from that consciousness.

---

[24]Compare Paul Tillich, "Rejoinder," 188.

The manner in which a symbol of being-itself participates in the reality it points to is a fundamentally different situation. There is a kind of participation involved here, and it does include the communication of power, but the power communicated by religious symbols is not a matter simply of one's reacting to a symbol as one would react to its referent. What is encountered here is, of course, the phenomenon of religious empowerment. Being-itself—that to which a religious symbol points—is not an entity, and the power experienced through a symbol of being-itself is not a participation in some power existing in and of itself apart from one's consciousness[25] nor an imitation of it. The representative religious symbol—the immediate, concrete object of ultimate concern—opens consciousness to being-itself; the religious symbol is "a symbol for a special relationship of the human mind to its own ultimate ground and meaning,"[26] in that it directs consciousness beyond that negation of being by nonbeing that threatens the self-world structure of being. By doing so it makes possible a phenomenon such as courage, which is the actual negation of the threat of nonbeing.

Symbols
Cannot Be Created at Will

The element of original affinity entails that symbols, unlike signs, are not arbitrary. Furthermore, one cannot simply decide to create a symbol. Tillich emphasizes that the origin of a symbol depends upon the "unconscious-conscious" reaction of a group.[27] Therefore, much of the element of affinity is a matter of affinity for a particular group of persons at a particular time in a particular situation. The collective experiences of a group will determine that certain objects or concepts, because of the connotations they have assumed through the group's experiences, automatically

---

[25]See the discussion of the four sub-roles of representative symbols in chapter 1 above.

[26]Tillich, "The Nature of Religious Language," 59.

[27]Tillich, "The Meaning and Justification of Religious Symbols," 4.

possess a symbolic quality.[28] Thus, as Tillich puts it, "a symbol is born and may die."[29] In other words, when a group's situation changes, some object or concept may suddenly attain symbolic significance or some previously symbolic object or concept may lose it.

The Correlation
of Reality and the Human Spirit

Representative symbols can create an awareness of dimensions of reality that correlate with dimensions of the human spirit, dimensions that otherwise would be unavailable to consciousness. The proper object of religion can be given to consciousness only in symbols, but Tillich holds that there are other realities available only through symbols. His assertion that art is symbolic clarifies this thought.

> You can take that which a landscape of Rubens, for instance, mediates to you. You cannot have this experience in any other way than through this painting made by Rubens. This landscape has some heroic character; it has character of balance, of colors, of weights, of values, and so on. All this is very external. What this mediates to you cannot be expressed in any other way than through this painting itself.[30]

The Rubens landscape reveals aspects of the natural world that one would be unaware of without the painting's mediation. And if a hitherto unseen dimension of the external world is opened up by this painting, so is a special dimension of the self, for "artistic symbols—in fact, all artistic creations—open up the human spirit for the dimension of aesthetic experience."[31] As the Rubens landscape demonstrates, symbols provide a

---

[28]Note that Tillich does use the Jungian phrase "collective unconscious." See "The Nature of Religious Language," 58; *Dynamics of Faith*, 43.

[29]Tillich, "The Meaning and Justification of Religious Symbols," 4.

[30]Tillich, "The Nature of Religious Language," 57.

[31]Tillich, "The Meaning and Justification of Religious Symbols," 5.

unique vision of the world and thereby open up a new dimension of the experiencing self.

Integrating and Disintegrating Power

Like participation, this fifth characteristic of representative symbols pertains to the phenomenon of empowerment; for Tillich claims that all representative symbols, not just religious symbols, can effect changes in consciousness, either for good or for ill. He states that

> this function of symbols refers both to individuals and groups. The history of religion gives an endless number of examples for the elevating, quieting, and stabilizing power of religious symbols. In the larger, and sometimes even narrower, sense of the word, one can speak of the "healing" power of religious symbols. All this is equally true of the three other groups of representative symbols. But in contrast to their integrating function, symbols can also have a disintegrating effect: causing restlessness, producing depression, anxiety, fanaticism, etc. This depends partly on the character of that to which they point, partly on the reaction of those who are grasped by them. Symbols have the same creative and destructive effect on social groups. Symbols are the main power of integrating them: a king, an event, a document in the political realm of representative symbolism, an epic work, architectural symbols, a holy figure, a holy book, a holy rite in religion. But here also are disintegrating possibilities as in some political symbols such as the Führer and the swastika, or in religious symbols such as the Moloch type of gods, human sacrifices, doctrinal symbols producing a split consciousness, etc. This characteristic of symbols shows their tremendous power of creation and destruction. By no means are they harmless semantic expressions.[32]

The creative and destructive power of symbols stems primarily from participation (with religious symbols—symbols of being-itself—participating in a unique fashion in that which they symbolize).

---

[32]Ibid., 5-6.

Testing the Truth
of Symbols

Genuine religious symbols "provide no objective knowledge, but yet a true awareness."[33] A religious symbol provides no information about being-itself but represents being-itself; it stands in for it as a concrete object of consciousness and thereby allows one to actualize a "special relationship" between one's consciousness and "its [consciousness's] own ultimate ground and meaning."[34] It has been suggested that when, in a further step, a symbol is experienced as the source of a power transcending the structure of being, being-itself is given to consciousness. If this suggestion is true, it implies that the phenomenon of empowerment guarantees that the symbol-produced awareness is a genuine awareness of being-itself. Is empowerment an infallible test of the truth of religious symbols? One must explore the body of Tillich's remarks on the truth of religious symbols in order to answer this question.

Tillich sees adequacy, self-negation, and quality of symbolic material as affecting a symbol's truth.[35] First,

> if one asks about criteria of religious symbols we must state generally that the measure of their validity is their adequacy to the religious experience they express. This is the basic criterion of all symbols. One can call it their "authenticity." Nonauthentic are religious symbols which have lost their experiential basis, but which are still used for reasons of tradition or because of their aesthetic value.[36]

Adequacy—authenticity—pertains to the use of the religious symbol, not as the concrete object of an ultimate concern that makes that concern possible, but to the subsequent use of the symbol to communicate the nature of that ultimate concern. Tillich further observes that "the criterion of au-

---

[33]Tillich, "The Religious Symbol," 316.

[34]Tillich, "The Nature of Religious Language," 59.

[35]See "The Meaning and Justification of Religious Symbols," 10-11.

[36]Ibid., 10.

thenticity is valid but not sufficient. It does not answer the question of the amount of truth a symbol possesses." In other words, adequacy does not guarantee that a symbol "reaches the referent" of a genuine religious symbol.[37]

How, then, does the self-negation of a symbol affect its truth? Self-negation pertains to how well a symbol negates its own importance while still pointing toward its referent. Sometimes the concrete contents of a symbol, the characteristics providing an affinity with being-itself, are themselves elevated to the level of the ultimate. They no longer merely stand in for what is ultimate. For instance, a statue located at a religious shrine is supposed to point beyond itself to the divine, but the statue may itself become an object of worship and be treated as of unconditional value. This situation exemplifies the danger of idolatry, which constantly plagues religious symbols. It is a danger that leads Tillich to assert that

> the criterion of the truth of faith, therefore, is that it implies an element of self-negation. That symbol is most adequate which expresses not only the ultimate but also its own lack of ultimacy. Christianity expresses itself in such a symbol in contrast to all other religions, namely, in the Cross of the Christ. Jesus could not have been the Christ without sacrificing himself as Jesus to himself as the Christ. Any acceptance of Jesus as the Christ which is not the acceptance of Jesus the crucified is a form of idolatry. The ultimate concern of the Christian is not Jesus, but the Christ Jesus who is manifest in the crucified.[38]

But while the cross's self-negation may help to prevent idolatry, self-negation's merely formal character—self-negation is an aspect of *how* the

---

[37]Ibid. Tillich sometimes speaks of adequacy as if it were directly connected with empowerment: " 'Adequacy' of expression means the power of expressing an ultimate concern in such a way that it creates reply, action, communication" (see *Dynamics of Faith*, 96). But note that, here too, adequacy has to do with *expressing* an ultimate concern. In other words, Tillich seems to be dealing with the symbol as a means of describing an ultimate concern, not as a means of "representation." If this is so, then adequacy is not related to the phenomenon of empowerment. However, there is ambiguity in Tillich's discussion of this matter, since he appears to go on to identify symbols with the "contents of ultimate concern" (see *Dynamics of Faith*, 96).

[38]Tillich, *Dynamics of Faith*, 97-98.

symbol works and does not necessarily determine *what* the symbol gives to consciousness—eliminates it as a test of whether a symbol mediates being-itself to consciousness. That is, the element of self-negation does not guarantee that, for a particular person, the symbol of the cross will provide a true awareness of being-itself: the cross may not be a live symbol for some persons, and in the future it may not be a live symbol for anyone. The formal characteristics of a symbol cannot guarantee that it will function as a religious symbol for a specific individual.[39] Tillich himself later admits that even the symbol of the cross "has become again and again the tool of idolatry within the Christian churches."[40]

In addition to adequacy and self-negation, Tillich discusses the quality of symbolic material as a criterion of its truth:

> There is a difference whether they use trees and rocks and stones and animals or personalities and groups as symbolic material. Only in the last case do the symbols comprise the whole of reality; for only in man are all dimensions of the encountered world united. It is therefore decisive for the rank and value of a symbol that its symbolic material is taken from the human person. Therefore, the great religions are concentrated on a personal development in which ultimate concern appears and transcends the personal limits, though remaining in a person. The positive criterion for the truth of a symbol (e.g., creation) is the degree in which it includes the valuation in an ultimate perspective of the individual persons.[41]

The first problem with this criterion is that Tillich's explanation of it is ambiguous. He seems at first to suggest that a symbol must be a person in order to represent being-itself effectively, as when the person of Jesus as the Christ or the concept of the personal God is used as a symbol. But Tillich's last sentence of the preceding quotation seems to shift emphasis so

---

[39]There is an important but different sense in which that formal quality does guarantee the symbol's truth: the symbol of the cross can be interpreted as a symbol that anticipates its own rejection, so that either an affirmation of the symbol or a rejection of it as a meaningful symbol confirms its truth. See Scharlemann, *Reflection and Doubt in the Thought of Paul Tillich*, 176-82.

[40]Tillich, "The Meaning and Justification of Religious Symbols," 10-11.

[41]Ibid., 11.

that he seems to suggest that to represent being-itself effectively, a symbol must include the *valuation of* the personal dimension of human being. Presumably, a tree when used as a symbol could be interpreted as including such a valuation. Furthermore, Tillich states elsewhere that when apersonal objects are used as symbols they can be interpreted as having personal qualities.[42]

But the main problem in using this criterion as a valid test of whether a symbol effects awareness of being-itself is that, like the criterion of self-negation, it is purely formal. Thus, it does not guarantee that, for a particular person, a certain symbol will produce a consciousness of being-itself.

If formal criteria can never guarantee that a religious symbol will in a particular situation mediate an awareness of being-itself, can one determine from how a particular person in a specific situation actually experiences a symbol whether that symbol is providing a true awareness? Is there something about the character of that experience that might guarantee that being-itself is being given to consciousness? The question here, in other words, is not whether there is a way to guarantee in advance that a symbol will mediate being-itself, but whether the actual use of a symbol can be tested.

One might suppose that the experience of the holiness of a symbol guaranteed its genuineness. Holiness is the "quality" that characterizes the content of ultimate concern.[43] Tillich draws upon Rudolph Otto's analysis of the holy as *mysterium fascinans et tremendum*, explaining that the reason for these two effects of the holy lies in the nature of ultimate concern.

> The human heart seeks the infinite because that is where the finite wants to rest. In the infinite it sees its own fulfillment. This is the reason for the ecstatic attraction and fascination of everything in which ultimacy is manifest. On the other hand, if ultimacy is manifest and exercises its fascinating attraction, one realizes at the same time the infinite distance of the finite from the infinite and, consequently, the negative judgment over any finite attempts to reach the infinite. The feeling of being con-

---

[42]Tillich, *Biblical Religion and the Search for Ultimate Reality*, 22-26.

[43]*ST*, 1:215.

sumed in the presence of the divine is a profound expression of man's relation to the holy.[44]

The character of the holy as *mysterium fascinans et tremendum* can be read as a manifestation of being-itself, for the extremes of fascinating and repelling suggest the unconditional character of the holy; no defining characteristics can be assigned to the holy, and it can be described only with simultaneously applied opposites. Tillich sees the following implications in Otto's analysis:

> When he points to the mysterious character of holiness, he indicates that the holy transcends the subject-object structure of reality. When he describes the mystery of the holy as *tremendum* and *fascinosum*, he expresses the experience of "the ultimate" in the double sense of that which is the abyss and that which is the ground of man's being.[45]

What is more, the experience of the holy is a matter of immediate certainty: "Faith is certain in so far as it is an experience of the holy."[46]

But the immediate certainty of holiness is not a guarantee that a symbol is providing a genuine awareness of being-itself. The quality of holiness accrues to *whatever* becomes an object of ultimate concern—"What concerns one ultimately becomes holy"[47]—and ultimate concerns are often misplaced, that is, focused upon a reality that does not point beyond itself to being-itself. The subjective aspect of ultimate concern bestows the quality of holiness upon any reality that becomes of ultimate concern. Holiness, in other words, is a function of the human act of concern rather than of the essence of the object of concern. The certainty and unconditionality of the holy flow from the nature of the human act of ultimate concern and belong to it alone.

> Only certain is the ultimacy as ultimacy, the infinite passion as infinite passion. This is a reality given to the self with his own nature. It is as immediate and as much beyond doubt as the self is to the self. It *is* the self in its self-transcending quality. But there is not certainty of this kind

---

[44]Tillich, *Dynamics of Faith*, 13.

[45]*ST*, 1:215-16.

[46]Tillich, *Dynamics of Faith*, 16.

[47]Ibid., 12-13.

about the content of our ultimate concern, be it nation, success, a god, or the God of the Bible: They all are contents without immediate awareness. Their acceptance as matters of ultimate concern is a risk.[48]

The risk is great, for if one is ultimately concerned about something that is not really ultimate, the object of concern may at some point display its lack of ultimacy; one then realizes that the basis of the meaning of one's life has been an illusion. Take, for example, a person who identifies with a nationalistic movement and elevates it to a level of ultimate concern. If the nationalistic hopes are shattered, the meaning of this person's being will be threatened.[49]

Thus, the experience of the holy is unsuitable as a test of whether a symbol provides an awareness of being-itself. But another candidate suggests itself: the phenomenon of empowerment. From what has been shown of it, may one not conclude that a symbol effecting religious empowerment must be a genuine symbol of being-itself? The answer to this question is both yes and no. Affirmatively, whenever a symbol does mediate being-itself to consciousness it can be an empowering symbol. Is the reverse also true? Can it be said that a symbol effecting religious empowerment—empowerment transcending the structure of being—provides an awareness of being-itself? Yes.

It has been shown that the experience of the holy entails a perception of the object of ultimate concern as unconditional, as representing the ground and abyss of being. But this perception turned out to be a function of the subjective side of ultimate concern—the human act of concern. The infinite passion of religious concern necessarily bestows these qualities upon its object. Is empowerment different? Might not the power of courage, for example, be caused by one's own subjectivity?

Holiness and empowerment are distinguishable in this regard. True, both occur within consciousness, but even in a phenomenological ontol-

---

[48]Ibid., 17. Compare Tillich's assertion that mere phenomenological description in the style of Otto's analysis of the holy must be augmented with a critique, since it cannot raise the question of the validity of the phenomena it describes. See "The Meaning and Justification of Religious Symbols," 7; *ST*, 1:106-108. The kind of phenomenology Tillich is criticizing here is of a purely eidetic variety and different from the transcendental kind that underlies his own ontology.

[49]See Tillich, *Dynamics of Faith*, 17-18.

ogy such as Tillich's, subjective elements can be distinguished from objective. The primary condition for the possibility of human consciousness is, after all, a structure containing an object pole over against a subjective pole. Holiness is a quality attributed to the concrete objects of ultimate concern, but it is bestowed upon objects by a subject; it is a function of the infinite passion, which is the subjective pole of ultimate concern. Thus, it lies on the self side of Tillich's self-world structure. Religious empowerment, on the other hand, is not a matter of the self or the world pole. In the phenomenon of courage, for example, one experiences the negating of the negation of being that characterizes the self-world structure of finite being. Courage, then, is not a matter of objects standing over against subjects, but of a dialectic transcending the structure in which objects and subjects stand over against one another. Thus, their different positions within the structure that is the condition for the possibility of human consciousness distinguishes holiness and religious empowerment.

On Tillich's terms, then, the experience of religious empowerment is an experience of a power transcending the self-world structure. Therefore, that power must be being-itself. Any symbol acting as the source of religious empowerment must be providing an awareness of being-itself. Several of Tillich's remarks confirm this conclusion. Regarding courage, he says,

> Every act of courage is a manifestation of the ground of being, however questionable the content of the act may be. The content may hide or distort true being, the courage in it reveals true being. Not arguments but the courage to be reveals the true nature of being-itself. . . . Courage has revealing power, the courage to be is the key to being-itself.[50]

And while Tillich believes that a religion like Christianity is not a theoretical proposition and thus cannot be verified in a detached, scientific manner, he suggests that if participation in a religion results in a certain type of empowerment, the truth of that religion has been validated: "Christianity can be called a hypothesis only in the large sense that the Christian faith includes an element of risk, and that it is subject to the continuous test of the power to overcome existential estrangement."[51] That

---

[50]Tillich, *The Courage to Be*, 181.

[51]Tillich, "Reply to Interpretation and Criticism," 383.

is, Christianity's truth is confirmed by its evocation of the power of being that overcomes the distortion of the structure of being characteristic of "fallenness."

However, there are two problems with affirming unequivocally that empowerment is an infallible sign of the truth of a symbol. First, although an instance of empowerment can be analyzed as to whether it entails a dialectical movement beyond the structure of being and thus is a manifestation of being-itself, few persons are equipped to make such an analysis. A person embracing a religious symbol might experience empowerment but might not possess the Tillichian tools necessary for analyzing the precise character and implications of that experience.

Second, the results of the requisite analysis—if one is skilled enough to make it—might be ambiguous. Consider once more the phenomenon of courage. Courage is a matter of self-affirmation, specifically, of self-affirmation over against the threat of nonbeing or in spite of it. Suppose that one does engage in an act of self-affirmation. A Tillichian analysis will show that the intent of this act is to counter nonbeing. But is this act of self-affirmation genuine, or is it a neurotic self-affirmation in which one affirms only a single, limited dimension of one's being, a dimension one has fled to in retreat from anxiety?[52] This question could not be answered unambiguously in every case. Tillich's analysis of that courage produced by the symbol of God, for example, must be seen as the distillation of the many experiences that constitute an entire religious tradition. There is no guarantee that in a particular case the results of an analysis would be unambiguous.

Thus, the phenomenon of religious empowerment guarantees that the symbol effecting it is mediating an awareness of being-itself. But it is not always clear whether in a given situation religious empowerment is occurring. The symbol may be providing a true awareness, but one cannot be certain that it is.

---

[52]Compare Tillich, *The Courage to Be*, 64-70.

3

Correlation
as a Hermeneutical Method

Being-itself possesses no positive, nonrelational attributes. It is inconceivable: one cannot comprehend what it is; positive, nonrelational concepts cannot be predicated of it. Yet being-itself can be symbolized, and not only by making figurative negative and relational statements about it, but through what here has been termed "representation." But a problem remains: can a symbol that does not describe any positive and nonrelational characteristics of its referent be interpreted? Is there any way to describe literally not only its figurative material but what it represents? Not that one should try to exhaust the function of a symbol, that is, replace it by way of a literal translation of its meaning; no effective symbol can ever be so reduced. But to interpret a symbol one must be able to describe literally what it gives to consciousness. One can, of course, always say of a genuine religious symbol that it represents being-itself. But this description hardly suffices. What about all of the apparent differences between religious symbols? Even when dealing with a single religious tradition, as Tillich is in the *Systematic Theology*, there are still distinctions to be made. One wants to be able to interpret the various symbols within that tradition in a manner allowing specification of how the symbol of the Christ, for example, gives to consciousness something different from what the symbol of God the Father does. Christian theologians surely do not want to be reduced to simply passing along the symbols of their tradition without comment. Such a procedure would not count as theology at all. Hence, this quandary: how to interpret representative religious symbols, to advance some sort of literal description of what they give to consciousness, when, because positive nonrelational predicates do not apply to being-itself, no such description is available (other than the bare description that all religious symbols represent being-itself).

I wish to argue that if a particular dimension of Tillich's method of correlation is employed, religious symbols can be interpreted. Tillich describes his method of correlation as the juxtaposition of "philosophical" or "existential" questions with religious symbols that answer them. His systematic theology "makes an analysis of the human situation out of which the existential questions arise, and it demonstrates that the symbols used in the Christian message are the answers to these questions."[1] Tillich's description of the purpose of his method of correlation suggests an apologetic goal: "The 'method of correlation' applied in the present system gives pointed expression to the decisive character of the apologetic element in systematic theology."[2] That is, it is assumed that philosophical questions express a particular cultural situation; if the Christian religious symbols can be shown to answer those questions, the apologetic task of the church has been accomplished. However, in addition to this explicit, acknowledged, *apologetic* method of correlation, there is implicit within Tillich's system what will be called a *hermeneutical* method of correlation.

Of course, the apologetic method of correlation is itself "hermeneutical" in that it is a means of "interpreting" religious symbols. But its interpretive function is, in the context of the problem under discussion here, less direct: the apologetic method of correlation—Tillich's explicit method—seeks to persuade one that the Christian symbols are relevant to one's situation; to adapt the symbols to a particular situation is to interpret them. But what is being called here the hermeneutical method of cor-

---

[1]*ST*, 1:62.

[2]Ibid., 31. Compare Paul Tillich, "The Problem of Theological Method," *Journal of Religion* 27 (1947): 25.

relation is interpretive in that it describes literally the contents of the symbols. It is, in other words, a method of correlation that can remedy the quandary posed earlier: it is a means of interpreting representative symbols of being-itself. With this method the philosophical questions and religious symbols are juxtaposed not as the expression of a cultural situation over against the Christian message, but as the expression of the structure of being over against being-itself as the depth of that structure.

Tillich himself agreed with Robert Scharlemann's formulation that "religious assertions are symbolic (referring to the depth of being), ontological assertions are literal (referring to the structure of being), and theological assertions are literal descriptions of the correlation between the religious symbols and the ontological concepts."[3] This formulation not only clarifies theology's role as a second-order operation upon the philosophical (or "ontological") component and religious component of the method of correlation—which make up questions and answers respectively—but also brings to light the ontological-structural relationship existing between the philosophical questions and the religious answers—the relationship the hermeneutical method of correlation presupposes.

I move now to a description of the mechanics of this hermeneutical version of the method of correlation. I shall argue that the phenomenon of empowerment is an essential element. My description will be augmented by a comparison of the structure of the hermeneutical correlation with that of the apologetic correlation. Next will come an investigation of the use of Tillich's implicit, hermeneutical correlation in the three major sections of the *Systematic Theology*. Then I shall consider the secondary literature on Tillich's method of correlation and explore the relevance of the secondary literature to a grasp of this hermeneutical method of correlation implicit in Tillich's system. Finally, I shall summarize the role played by empowerment in Tillich's theology.

---

[3]Robert P. Scharlemann, "Tillich's Method of Correlation: Two Proposed Revisions," *Journal of Religion* 46 (January 1966): 93. On p. 184 of his "Rejoinder" in the same issue, Tillich expresses his agreement and goes on to admit that he has sometimes blurred these distinctions. For example, sometimes he speaks of correlation as a juxtaposition of philosophical questions and *theological* answers instead of *religious* answers. See *ST*, 1:60.

The Implicit, Hermeneutical Correlation

How is it that Tillich successfully carries out the hermeneutical assignment that faces him? His implicit, hermeneutical method of correlation provides an *indirect* description of what religious symbols give to consciousness, thereby avoiding a futile attempt to provide a direct description of being-itself as the object of symbolic representation.

It has been noted that Tillich most often describes his method of correlation as a matter of questioning and answering. Now, the juxtaposition of religious symbols with the questions those symbols answer is itself a process of interpretation, for it provides an indirect description of what the symbols communicate. That is, nothing is said directly about being-itself as the object of the symbols, yet information is provided about how the symbols function. In order to understand more fully how this process works, the phenomenon of empowerment must be considered.

How can a religious symbol be said to answer a particular question if it provides no positive description of that which it symbolizes? While philosophically analyzing human being, one might ask, "What is the source of courage?" One might then answer that being-itself is the source, and that one is made aware of it through a religious symbol. But, granting that the symbol provides an awareness of being-itself, can it be said to answer the question? It is, after all, *only* an awareness that the symbol provides; it does not evoke statements that can be said to answer a theoretical query. What needs to be understood here, however, is that Tillich does not have theoretical questions in mind, questions that seek information. Rather, he thinks in terms of questions that are expressions of a longing. Thus, in this context, when one asks, "What is the source of courage?" what is sought is not information about the source of courage, but the source itself in the sense of longing to make contact with it. In other words, the existential questions that form one-half of Tillich's method of correlation are questions asking *for* something rather than questions asking *about* something,[4] a fact evident from Tillich's characterization of correlation:

----

[4]See Alistair M. Macleod, *Paul Tillich: An Essay on the Role of Ontology in his Philosophical Theology* (London: George Allen and Unwin, 1973) 32ff.

The answers implied in the event of revelation are meaningful only in so far as they are in correlation with questions concerning the whole of our existence, with existential questions. Only those who have experienced the shock of transitoriness, the anxiety in which they are aware of their finitude, the threat of nonbeing, can understand what the notion of God means. Only those who have experienced the tragic ambiguities of our historical existence and have totally questioned the meaning of existence, can understand what the symbol of the Kingdom of God means. Revelation answers questions which have been asked and always will be asked because they are "we ourselves."[5]

Thus, it becomes clear how the empowering quality of religious symbols equips them to "answer" certain questions. As David Kelsey has observed,

> the "answer" is not a statement given in response to a request for information. It is rather the power that brings cessation to a personal quest for ontological healing. The content of the biblical symbols' "answer" is not stateable information or advice, but a power.[6]

Kelsey's observations do not completely explain, however, how the phenomenon of empowerment allows interpretation of religious symbols, for it would be easy to misconceive the hermeneutical role of empowerment so as to overlook the indirectness of Tillich's method. Note that in the phenomenon of religious empowerment, the power itself—that is, the reality of being-itself that is given to consciousness—can be distinguished from the empirical effect of that power within the structure of finite being. Now, the direct meaning of the symbol, that which it represents and gives to consciousness, is the first of these—being-itself as the power of being. But to assert that the direct meaning of a religious symbol is being-itself is hardly a sufficient interpretation of it, since being-itself cannot be described positively and nonrelationally. If this were all one could say in interpreting a religious symbol, the same brief interpretation would have to be applied to every genuine religious symbol: it represents the power of being-itself.

---

[5]*ST*, 1:61-62.

[6]David H. Kelsey, *The Uses of Scripture in Recent Theology* (Philadelphia: Fortress Press, 1975) 72.

On the other hand, the empirically available effect of the power of being within the structure of finitude—the healing of the disrelation between the polar elements, for instance—is not the meaning of the symbol either. To believe so is to attempt another sort of direct interpretation: one cannot translate a religious symbol by simply describing the reality the symbol represents, so one reduces the whole content of the symbol to what it is observed to effect; one undertakes a kind of pragmatic translation. This is clearly an errant procedure, for the symbol symbolizes not just this finite effect but the reality of being-itself.

The key to understanding Tillich's implicit, hermeneutical method is to take the notion of correlation seriously—that is, to understand that Tillich does not provide a direct account of the meaning of a religious symbol, but an indirect one. The import of the observable, finite component of the phenomenon of empowerment, then, is not that it exhausts the meaning of the symbol that is its source, but that it provides an objective datum by means of which one can juxtapose the symbol with the question it answers.

Recall that Tillich deals with different types of religious empowerment, three of which were mentioned in chapter 1: namely, courage as the negation of nonbeing's negation of being, the conquest of the disrelation between the polar elements that characterizes "fallenness," and the conquest of those ambiguities of language caused by the subject-object structure of all discourse. Now suppose that a particular religious symbol—for instance, following Tillich, the symbol of Jesus as the Christ—provides the power to overcome the disrelation between the polar elements of freedom and destiny. The observation that it does so allows one to interpret the symbol of the Christ, to give an indirect account of its meaning, by juxtaposing it with the question of how to transcend the conflict between freedom and destiny. More precisely, it allows one to "locate" that symbol in a particular region of human being as that region is described by Tillich's ontological analysis.[7] Another symbol—for instance, again following Tillich, the symbol of God—may empower courage. That symbol, then, thanks to the objective datum offered by the phenomenon of empower-

---

[7]Compare Robert Scharlemann's assertion that Tillich's intent is to "place" the symbols properly. *Reflection and Doubt in the Thought of Paul Tillich*, 136.

ment, can be correlated with a different question—it can be located in a different region of human being.

How does this ability to interpret different religious symbols differently concur with the representation of the same thing—namely, being-itself—by all religious symbols? Tillich's implicit, hermeneutical method of correlation allows one to interpret two separate symbols differently because it shows that each of the two symbols provides a distinctive perspective upon being-itself. Each of the symbols provides an awareness of being-itself from the perspective of a particular place within the structure of finite being.

This statement does not mean that what Tillich's indirect method of interpretation makes available is accidental to what is really represented by the symbol. What is available is not extrinsic in the way that the apparent convergence of two parallel lines at the horizon is extrinsic to the actual, objective relationship between the lines. Being-itself can be described only as that which lies beyond the structure of finite being, as the depth of the self-world structure. Being-itself is not a thing in itself, an object that can be thought of as existing independently of the structure of finitude in the way that the relationship between two lines exists independently of one's perceiving that relationship; the notion of being-itself requires the notion of the self-world structure as that which it is the depth of. Indeed, being-itself is given to consciousness as a power that dialectically overcomes a conflict between two poles of the structure of being. Thus, to specify the point within the structure of finitude from which a symbol offers a view of being-itself is not to refer to something that lies outside the nature of what is being viewed. It would be different, of course, if one were specifying perspectival differences that could be traced to the idiosyncrasies of the individuals who embraced a particular symbol and the times and places in which they embraced it. What is being discussed, instead, are perspectival differences based upon differing components of the ontological structure.

Thus, Tillich is faced with the task of finding a way to interpret religious symbols meaningfully, symbols whose object is beyond conceptualization. A meaningful interpretation is one that can provide an account, not just of the figurative material employed in a symbol, but of that which is represented in the symbol. Such an interpretation must therefore be able to distinguish between different religious symbols. Tillich succeeds in this task by finding a way to describe indirectly what a religious symbol represents. He juxtaposes a particular symbol with the question it answers, thereby specifying the location within the ontological structure from which being-itself is viewed or given to consciousness. The juxtaposition of question and answer is made possible by the objective datum provided by the phenomenon of empowerment.

Hence, *the implicit, hermeneutical method of correlation gives an indirect interpretation of a religious symbol by locating it within the structure of being on the basis of the observable transformation it empowers.*

The Structures of the Apologetic and the Hermeneutical Correlation

Earlier, it was suggested that implied in Tillich's system is a hermeneutical method of correlation distinguishable from the more apparent apologetic correlation. That hermeneutical correlation was discussed above. But how does it differ from the apologetic method of correlation? To answer this question will further elucidate the character of Tillich's implicit, hermeneutical method of correlation.

The Apologetic Correlation

The structure of the apologetic correlation is based upon the relationship between philosophical questions and theological answers. While the answers are an expression of the "Christian message," the questions express what Tillich terms the "situation."[8] Now, "the 'situation' that theology must respond to is the totality of man's creative self-interpretation *in a special period.*"[9] Thus, the questions must express the perspective of the particular culture in which theologians find themselves. It is philosophy's role to generate these questions; the questions arise from a philosophical analysis of human being. Thus, philosophy's primary purpose in the apologetic correlation is to represent and articulate the concerns of the society toward whom the Christian message is to be directed. John Clayton

---

[8]*ST*, 1:3-6.

[9]Ibid., 4. Emphasis added.

explains how the notion of cultural situation comes to be equated with philosophy in the *Systematic Theology*:

> First, 'situation' is translated from the actual conditions under which people live at a given time and in a given place to their 'self-understanding': ' "Situation," as one pole of all theological work, does not refer to the psychological or sociological state in which individuals or groups live. It refers to the scientific and artistic, the economic, political, and ethical forms in which they express their interpretation of existence'. (ST. I. 3-4) That is to say, 'situation' is transformed into *ideology*. The next step is to reduce each of these various forms of expression to philosophy.[10]

Philosophy is primarily important in this case not as an expression of a particular dimension of every human being's consciousness but as an expression of a particular cultural situation.

The questions generated by a philosophical investigation are correlated with the symbols provided by the Christian faith. Since the questions are "existential" in nature, that is, an enunciation of the quest for the fulfillment of the meaning of human being, they are answered when the symbols empower courage as the conquest of the threat of nonbeing, the conquest of the disrelation of the polar elements, and the conquest of ambiguities such as those accompanying the use of language.

The reason for adopting the question-answer format in the apologetic version of correlation is that it can demonstrate the relevance of the Christian message to the present cultural situation; the goal is apologetic, that is, to show that Christianity does answer the questions most important to contemporary men and women, including present-day cultured despisers of religion. It follows that, while a theologian may, in setting up the correlation, begin with the symbols and then try to find the questions they answer, the actual movement of thought characterizing the apologetic correlation is indeed from question to answer.

The Hermeneutical Correlation

The structure of the implicit, hermeneutical correlation too, as has been shown, is based upon the relationship between questions and an-

---

[10]John P. Clayton, *The Concept of Correlation: Paul Tillich and the Possibility of a Mediating Theology* (Berlin: de Gruyter, 1980) 139.

swers. And, as with the apologetic method of correlation, the answers given in the hermeneutical method of correlation take the form of religious symbols. Here the similarity ends.

First, the purpose of the hermeneutical correlation is different: it is employed not in order to communicate the Christian message to the larger culture Christianity resides in, but to find a way to interpret or conceptualize symbols that represent an inconceivable reality. Thus, philosophy does not stand over against symbol as culture over against Christianity. Rather, philosophy, which generates the questions through an analysis of human being, is juxtaposed to symbol as an expression of the structure of being over against an expression of its depth. This means that the questions and answers thus represent two different dimensions *of an individual's consciousness.* Philosophy is reason operating within the self-world structure, while the awareness provided by religious symbols is an example of "ecstatic" reason, a type of reason that transcends the self-world structure.[11] In contrast, the apologetic method sees philosophical questions and religious answers as representing *two separate groups,* the culture and the church.

The depth of being cannot be described as the structure of being can, for the former is inconceivable, possessing no positive and nonrelational attributes. Thus, where the depth, that is, being-itself, is concerned, indirect description must be used. One *correlates* the structure of being, which is conceivable and describable, with the depth of being—juxtaposing them as question and answer. The motive for using the question-answer format in the hermeneutical correlation is to provide an indirect approach to religious symbols; the motive for using it in the apologetic correlation is to show that the Christian message answers the needs of contemporary society.

A further difference concerns the direction of thought involved in the hermeneutical correlation, a difference based on the differing goals of the hermeneutical and apologetic correlations. With the hermeneutical correlation, one begins with the symbol and moves to the question; what is important here is not that a symbol *answers* a question—the central point in the apologetic method—but *what* question it answers. One learns about what the symbol represents by investigating the nature of the particular question it answers; one looks back from answer to question.

------

[11]See *ST,* 1:111-15.

Of course, there are connections between the two methods of correlation. For example, even in the hermeneutical correlation, the manner in which the philosophical questions are formulated will reflect a cultural situation, although in the hermeneutical correlation this reflection is irrelevant.

A more important connection can be seen in Tillich's earlier work. There, he spends a good deal of time exploring the relationship between religion and culture—which obviously relates to the apologetic correlation—but he sees that relationship in ontological-structural terms—which suggests the implicit, hermeneutical correlation.

Here is a representative formulation from this early period: "der tragende Gehalt der Kultur ist die Religion, und die notwendige Form der Religion ist die Kultur."[12] Religion concerns the unconditional depth of the structure of being. That unconditional reality becomes an object for human consciousness through cultural forms that symbolize it. Culture is thus the *form* of religion. At the same time, religion is the unconditional source of meaning a culture draws upon; it is the *content* or *substance* of culture.[13] Thus, behind Tillich's discussion in the *Systematic Theology* of correlation as a juxtaposition of a cultural situation and Christian symbols (the apologetic correlation) there lies his earlier work on the *Form-Gehalt* relationship between culture and its unconditional depth. This relationship makes it easier to recognize that alongside the apologetic correlation in the *Systematic Theology* exists the implicit, hermeneutical correlation, with its ontological-structural orientation.

The Hermeneutical Correlation
in the Three Main Parts
of the *Systematic Theology*

The *Systematic Theology* is divided into the following five sections: "Reason and Revelation," "Being and God," "Existence and the Christ,"

---

[12]Quoted by Clayton, *The Concept of Correlation*, 191. The quotation comes from a 1924 essay entitled "Kirche und Kultur" and can be found in *Gesammelte Werke*, 9:42.

[13]On the translation of "*Gehalt*," see Scharlemann, *Reflection and Doubt in the Thought of Paul Tillich*, 36n.

"Life and the Spirit," and "History and the Kingdom of God." Tillich
points out, however, that the discussion of revelation and its relation to
reason—the topic of the first section—actually belongs to all other parts
of the system and is treated separately for practical reasons. Similarly, history—the topic of the fifth section—is a dimension of what Tillich terms
"life" and is treated separately from the section on life for practical reasons.[14] Thus, it can be said that there are three main parts of the *Systematic Theology*. Tillich describes them by saying,

> Man's predicament, out of which the existential questions arise, must
> be characterized by three concepts: finitude with respect to man's es-
> sential being as creature, estrangement with respect to man's existential
> being in time and space, ambiguity with respect to man's participation
> in life universal. The questions arising out of man's finitude are an-
> swered by the doctrine of God and the symbols used in it. The questions
> arising out of man's estrangement are answered by the doctrine of Christ
> and the symbols applied to it. The questions arising out of the ambi-
> guities of life are answered by the doctrine of the Spirit and its sym-
> bols.[15]

It is the third main section of Tillich's system, which deals with life
and its ambiguities, that describes what is experienced as the actuality of
the everyday. In contrast, the first two sections deal with abstractions from
this everyday experience—that is, with dimensions of experience unap-
parent at first, but revealed through analysis as implicit.

That Tillich's hermeneutical method of correlation is manifest in each
of these three main divisions of the *Systematic Theology* will be shown below.

Essential Being and God

There is a potential source of confusion in Tillich's use of the word
God. On the one hand, Tillich uses it as a term that, while operating within
the religious rather than the philosophical realm, parallels the term *being-
itself*. Tillich initiates his doctrine of God "by defining God as being-it-

---

[14]See *ST*, 1:66-67, 2:4.

[15]Ibid., 3:285-86.

self,"[16] and states that "the religious word for what is called the ground of being is God."[17] In other words, "God" is a term designating the inconceivable goal of the ontological question when that goal is experienced as one's ultimate concern.

On the other hand, Tillich uses the word *God* to denote a particular symbol: "God is the fundamental symbol for what concerns us ultimately."[18] He is explicit about this dual usage, asserting that

> we cannot simply say that God is a symbol. We must always say two things about him: we must say that there is a non-symbolic element in our image of God—namely, that he is ultimate reality, being-itself, ground of being, power of being; and the other, that he is the highest being in which everything that we have does exist in the most perfect way. If we say this we have in our mind the image of a highest being, a being with the characteristics of highest perfection. That means that we have a symbol for that which is not symbolic in the idea of God—namely, "Being-itself."[19]

Thus, "God is symbol for God."[20] The potential for confusion here is obvious,[21] and in order to avoid it, it is perhaps helpful to employ two designations for the two different senses of "God." Tillich himself sometimes does this: at certain points in his writing he calls God in the non-symbolic sense "the God above the God of theism."[22] Then it can be said that "the God of traditional theism is a symbol for the God beyond the

---

[16]Ibid., 2:10.

[17]Ibid., 1:156.

[18]Tillich, *Dynamics of Faith*, 46.

[19]Tillich, "The Nature of Religious Language," 61.

[20]Tillich, *Dynamics of Faith*, 46.

[21]Consider Tillich's difficulty in deciding whether "God is being-itself" is a completely nonsymbolic statement or one that is both symbolic and nonsymbolic. See *ST*, 1:238-39 and *ST*, 2:9-10. Compare Scharlemann, *Reflection and Doubt in the Thought of Paul Tillich*, 76-82.

[22]See Tillich, *The Courage to Be*, 182-90. Compare *ST*, 2:12.

God of theism."[23] In order to avoid confusion in the discussion that follows, God in the nonsymbolic sense will be called "the God above God" or "God as being-itself," while God in the symbolic sense will be called "the symbol of God" (understood as an appositive genitive) or "the Supreme Being."

In the discussion in the *Systematic Theology* of essential being and the doctrine of God, the task to which the hermeneutical correlation must be applied is the interpretation of the symbol of God as it is found in the Christian tradition. Tillich asserts that the symbol of God as found there empowers courage:

> Faith in the almighty God is the answer to the quest for a courage which is sufficient to conquer the anxiety of finitude. . . . When the invocation "Almighty God" is seriously pronounced, a victory over the threat of nonbeing is experienced, and an ultimate, courageous affirmation of existence is expressed.[24]

"Faith in the eternal God is the basis for a courage which conquers the negativities of the temporal process."[25] One necessarily seeks the courage that can conquer the anxiety of nonbeing, and "the question of God is the question of the possibility of this courage."[26] The dialectic involved in the experience of courage can be explained as follows: one seeks to secure a meaningful existence, to affirm one's being in the fullest sense of the word *being.* In opposition to this goal, one encounters nonbeing through anxiety—the awareness of a threat to one's being. But the arrival of courage means that one discovers oneself able to affirm the meaning of one's being in spite of the threat of nonbeing.

There are actually two ways of specifying how this phenomenon transcends the poles of the structure of finite being. First, the essence of finitude has been described by Tillich as being limited by nonbeing. Courage is the negation of nonbeing's negation of being. Hence, courage gives to

---

[23]Tillich, "Theology and Symbolism," 114. Compare Paul Tillich, "The God above God," in *The Listener* 66 (3 August 1961): 169, 172.

[24]*ST*, 1:273.

[25]Ibid., 276.

[26]Ibid., 198.

consciousness a power that lies beyond the structure of finitude. Second, this dialectic takes place within the structure of being as described by the four levels of ontological concepts. Thus, with regard to the second level of ontological concepts, for example, the threat of nonbeing is manifest in the ever-present possibility that the polar elements of freedom and destiny will break apart from one another. Courage involves the conquest of that threat and therefore depends upon a power transcending the polar structure of being; it depends upon the power that grounds the structure.

But whether one thinks of the two fundamental poles transcended in courage as nonbeing and being, or as elements described by one of the four levels of ontological concepts, what is being discussed is a form of religious empowerment that operates within the realm of *essential* being. That is to say, the religious empowerment represented by courage is not needed because the structure of being has been somehow undermined or distorted. Rather, this negation of the negation of being would have to occur even if the structure of being were as it essentially ought to be.

The symbol of God empowers courage, and courage is a manifestation of being-itself that is required within the context of essential being. On this basis the symbol of God can be correlated with the question "How is the courage of self-affirmation that is required to overcome the threat of nonbeing against being that characterizes the structure of finite being in its essence possible?" Thus, the Christian symbol of God is indirectly interpreted—is "located"—by saying that it provides a dialectical awareness of being-itself from the perspective of the structure of being qua *the structure of finite reality as it essentially ought to be* or qua *the basic condition of the possibility of human experience.*

If this account is accurate, then the implicit, hermeneutical method of correlation does offer a legitimate, albeit indirect, interpretation of the Christian symbol of God. But Tillich's discussion of the doctrine of God considers more than the basic Christian God-symbol as a single entity. What about the many permutations of this basic symbol?

Tillich's analysis of the Christian doctrine of God considers some of these permutations. His approach is systematic: he considers the different levels of the ontological structure, and by applying the concepts found on those different levels to God as being-itself, he establishes how particular variations of the symbol of God arise. The results are symbolic because these concepts cannot be predicated literally of God as being-itself; that is, the result is a number of variations on the concept of the Supreme Being.

Tillich begins with the level of the structure concerning the transition from essence to existence. There, God can be said to lie beyond the tension between essence and existence as well as beyond the duality of infinite and finite. Tillich next points out that God can be said to be living, in that he cannot be conceived of as a pure identity of being. Being-itself involves a continual dialectic, the negation of the negation of being. The character of this divine life, which is already a symbolic notion, can be further symbolized by drawing upon the three sets of polar elements. Utilizing the elements of individuation and participation, for example, it can be said that God is both a personal Supreme Being and a universal presence. And if God is thought of as the union of all the ontological elements plus the *telos* of life, it can be said that he is spirit.

Having considered the dimensions of the symbol of the living God, Tillich explores the symbols of God's relation to his creatures. Here he speaks of God's originating, sustaining, and directing creativity. Tillich explains that when one calls God the "creative ground" of being, one is drawing upon the categories of causality and substance, for the term suggests a reality transcending those two categories of finitude and the tensions between being and nonbeing manifested in them. With regard to the category of time this transcendence is expressed in the statement "God is eternal"; with regard to space it is expressed in the statement "God is omnipresent." The general symbol for God's transcendence of all the categories of finitude is the "almighty" or omnipotent God. The spiritual character of this transcendence, its relation to the subject-object structure through which reality is experienced, is expressed in the statement "God is omniscient." Concluding his description of God's relation to his creatures, Tillich discusses the symbols of God as love, as Lord, and as Father.[27] The first level of the ontological structure, the self-world polarity, cannot serve as the basis for symbols of God because self and world are kinds of being rather than qualities of being.[28]

There is an ambiguity to Tillich's discussion of the permutations of the basic Christian symbol of God, which makes uncovering the implicit, hermeneutical correlation at work in the *Systematic Theology* more com-

---

[27]This summary covers *ST*, 1:235-89.

[28]See ibid., 244.

plicated. Tillich here conflates a view of symbolic meaning interpretable through the hermeneutical correlation with a view that is not. Specifically, he fails to keep separate the lesser function of religious symbols—figuratively expressing negative and relational details about being-itself—and their essential function—"representation." Here are three ways of articulating the problem: Tillich conflates (a) a symbol with (b) a symbolic proposition, (a) the concrete content of an ultimate concern that provides a dialectical awareness of being-itself with (b) a negative or relational fact about being-itself figuratively expressed, and (a) an answer to a question asking *for* something with (b) an answer to a question asking *about* something.[29]

Take, for example, the idea of God as eternal: how can it be fitted into the hermeneutical correlation? According to this investigation thus far, the Christian symbol of God represents being-itself to consciousness in such a way that it empowers courage. But to speak simply of "the symbol of God" is to speak very generally. The symbol of God is actually a complex entity and can be understood as an aggregate symbol made up of numerous other symbols. It is the concept of the Supreme Being, used to represent the God beyond God: being-itself. Thus, the constituent symbols of this complex symbol turn out to be specific aspects of the concept of the Supreme Being. The symbol of the eternal God, in other words, is based upon the concept of the eternal Supreme Being, that is, a being not subject to the limitations characterizing essential temporality.[30]

This concept of an eternal Supreme Being has obvious negative affinities with being-itself and is thus well equipped to serve as a symbol of being-itself. What is more, the character of those affinities allows for its providing an awareness of being-itself from a very specific place within the structure of being. And indeed Tillich asserts, "Faith in the eternal God is the basis for a courage which conquers the negativities of the temporal process."[31] That is, faith in the eternal God overcomes the conflict between being and nonbeing that characterizes essential temporality.[32] Thus,

---

[29]Regarding the last of these three problems, see Macleod, *Paul Tillich*, 32ff.

[30]See *ST*, 1:192-94.

[31]Ibid., 276.

[32]Ibid., 192-93.

this constituent symbol of the basic Christian God-symbol can be located with great specificity: the symbol of the eternal God provides a dialectical awareness of being-itself from the perspective of the category of temporality in its essential state.

What, then, of the other approach employed by Tillich? The notion of God as eternal has been interpreted here as a symbol providing a dialectical awareness of being-itself and answering the quest for the courage to overcome a form of the threat of nonbeing. The notion of the eternal God—the eternal Supreme Being—is thus seen as the concrete content of an ultimate concern, a content that stands in for or represents being-itself. But, moving from symbol to symbolic assertion, suppose that one sets forth the proposition "God is eternal," or more exactly, "The God above God is the eternal Supreme Being." That a symbolic *sentence* rather than a symbolic *concept* or *object* is being dealt with here does not mean that the symbolic function involved is a matter of assertion rather than representation. Such a sentence communicates a concept that could have a representative function. But suppose it does not. Then the concept of the eternal Supreme Being no longer serves a symbolic function by *representing* or *standing in* for being-itself; instead, its symbolic function is served by expressing something *about* being-itself.

But only negative or relational assertions can be made about being-itself, and symbols are not necessary for making those assertions. While it is impossible to completely reduce such a symbolic proposition to a literal one because its figurative form may have some unique value in *how* it communicates the information—it may, for example, have a special value for piety—it is possible to translate the information itself into literal terms. Thus, the meaning of the symbolic proposition "The God above God is the eternal Supreme Being" could be expressed:

> The divine life includes temporality, but it is not subject to it. The divine eternity includes time and transcends it. The time of the divine life is determined not by the negative element of creaturely time but by the present, not by the "no longer" and the "not yet" of our time.[33]

This symbolic proposition, "The God above God is eternal," can be correlated with the question "What reality provides the courage that over-

---

[33]Ibid., 257.

comes the anxiety produced by the element of nonbeing in temporality?" in the sense not that it actually provides the reality being sought (that is, it is not the answer to a question asking *for* something), but in the sense that it provides negative or relational information about it (that is, it is the answer to a question asking *about* something).

This approach to symbolic meaning creates a contradiction in Tillich's work. On the one hand, he says that human consciousness of being-itself requires symbols. But it has just been shown that the information about being-itself communicated by a symbolic proposition can be translated into something other than a symbol; in fact, Tillich translates that particular proposition himself. This contradiction has not escaped Tillich's commentators and critics. Guyton Hammond observes:

> After having maintained that all language about God is symbolic and not to be judged in terms of its literal truth or falsity, Tillich proceeds to a very subtle and intricate metaphysical analysis of the divine nature. It is always difficult for the reader to remember that this analysis is to be considered symbolic, not literally true.[34]

William Alston is more specific and critical:

> As his own principles demand, Tillich explicitly disavows any intent to interpret a religious symbol by specifying the aspect of the Ultimate to which it points. "Every symbol opens up a level of reality for which non-symbolic speaking is inadequate" ("Religious Symbols and Our Knowledge of God," *The Christian Scholar* 38:191). And yet when Tillich actually goes about explaining various theological terms, it looks very much as if he is trying to translate them into ontological terms. . . . "If we call God the 'living God' . . . we assert that he is the eternal process in which separation is posited and is overcome by reunion" (ST1:242). . . . "Will and intellect in their application to God . . . are symbols for dynamics in all its ramifications and for form as the meaningful structure of being-itself" (ST1:247). . . . "It is more adequate to define divine omnipotence as the power of being which resists nonbeing in all its expressions and which is manifest in the creative process in all its forms"

---

[34]Hammond, *The Power of Self-Transcendence*, 119.

> (ST1:273). . . . I do not know how to read this other than as an attempt
> to translate symbolic language into nonsymbolic language.[35]

Indeed, Tillich is interpreting symbolic propositions by translating them into literal statements of negative and relational facts about being-itself. Read in their context the first two examples cited by Alston concern the fact that the God above God, as being-itself, transcends the polar elements of finite being. He "contains" these elements within himself and is not determined by them. The third example simply expresses the relation of God as being-itself to finitude; he is the negation of the negation of being.

Why does Tillich transgress his own dictum that one ought not try to reduce symbols to literal statements? Because he is surreptitiously employing two different senses of symbolic meaning. On the one hand is the symbol that serves as a concrete content of an ultimate concern. It does not provide facts about being-itself but, rather, represents being-itself to consciousness in the technical sense of "representation" discussed in chapters 1 and 2 and provides a dialectical awareness of being-itself. No translation or reduction is possible here, only an indirect account via the implicit, hermeneutical method of correlation. On the other hand is the symbolic proposition, whose whole function is to figuratively express negative or relational facts about being-itself. Such symbolic propositions can be directly translated into nonsymbolic form.

The existence of this second type of symbolic meaning in the *Systematic Theology* illuminates once more the difference between the apologetic and hermeneutical correlation. In the hermeneutical correlation, the correlation itself is the interpretive moment of the discussion; it is the indirect location of a symbol vis-à-vis the philosophical-conceptual sphere. But in the apologetic correlation, the correlation itself interprets the symbol only in the sense of demonstrating its relevance to a particular cultural situation. Thus, after the moment of correlation, a means of literally expressing its conceptual content is still necessary. The interpretation of a symbol as a symbolic proposition that can be converted into a negative or relational literal statement about being-itself is the fruit of this requirement.

---

[35]Alston, "Tillich's Conception of a Religious Symbol," 25. I have changed the page numbers that Alston cites to the corresponding pages in the edition of *ST* 1 that I have been citing.

The conflation of the two functions of symbol within the *Systematic Theology* may have several causes. First, both functions are legitimate (though the representative function is essential to consciousness of being-itself while the informational function is not). And when one recalls that one formulation can bear both functions, the potential for confusion is obvious. It has been shown, for example, how the notion of the eternal Supreme Being can be understood either as a representative symbol or as a symbolic proposition communicating negative and relational facts. The manner in which it should be understood cannot be determined by its outward form. In other words, a symbol might take the form of the proposition "God is eternal." But because a symbol's outward form is propositional does not mean its function must be propositional or informational, as opposed to representational, for that proposition communicates the concept of the eternal Supreme Being that in turn can stand in, in the sense of representation, for being-itself.

Another possible source of confusion arises from the distinction made between asking *about*, to which the informational or propositional function of a symbol corresponds, and asking *for*, which the representational function answers. John Clayton has pointed out that the distinction between the two types of asking is easily blurred in German, since either type can be spoken of as "eine Frage nach." Thus, Tillich's native tongue may have contributed to his moving back and forth between asking about and asking for without his noticing the change.[36]

Existence and the Christ

The event that lies at the heart of the Christian faith, the event of Jesus as the Christ, is, Tillich says, a composite of two major components: "Jesus as the Christ is both a historical fact and a subject of believing reception."[37] In other words, on the one hand there is a historical fact, that is, the life and death of a particular individual identified in the New Testament as Jesus of Nazareth. On the other hand there is a particular community's reception of this individual as a bearer of salvific power. The

---

[36]Clayton, *The Concept of Correlation*, 180-81.

[37]*ST*, 2:98.

believing-reception component of the event is manifested in what Tillich terms "the picture of Jesus as the Christ" contained in the New Testament.[38] This picture is made up, among other elements, of stories, symbols out of Jewish tradition such as "Son of Man" and "Christ" ("Messiah"), and new symbols such as "the cross of the Christ" and "the resurrection of the Christ." But this picture is a unified whole and is to be understood as itself a symbol, a symbol that empowers what Tillich terms "New Being." Indeed, while uncertainty is connected with the historical-fact component of the event of Jesus as the Christ—Tillich claims that, although one can know that there was a person who was the bearer of the New Being, one cannot be certain that his name was Jesus, that he was from Nazareth, and so forth—it is certain that the New Testament picture of the Christ, the receptive, symbolic side of the event, has transforming power.[39]

To discover that the picture or symbol of Jesus as the Christ empowers New Being is the first step in interpreting that symbol by means of the implicit, hermeneutical correlation. Tillich explains that "New Being is essential being under the conditions of existence, conquering the gap between essence and existence."[40] New Being overcomes the distortion of essential being that can be termed "fallen" being or "estrangement."[41] What, precisely, is the character of this distortion? On the first and most basic level of the ontological structure, estrangement from the ground of being is manifest as self-loss and world-loss.

Self-loss is the loss of one's determining center, the disintegration of the

———————

[38]See ibid., 102ff.

[39]See ibid., 107-17.

[40]Ibid., 118.

[41]Tillich actually begins his treatment of the doctrine of the Christ with what he calls "the symbol of 'the fall' " rather than with the symbol of the Christ (see *ST*, 2:29-44). But the Fall is not a *religious* symbol in the technical sense that it represents being-itself. Instead, it represents a distortion of being resulting from estrangement from being-itself. Because it is true that, in Tillich's words, "in order to understand any distortion, one must know its undistorted or essential character" (*ST*, 2:4), one could say that the Fall is a symbol that is parasitic on another symbol, a religious one, such as the symbol of the Christ or the symbol of God.

unity of the person. This is manifest in moral conflicts and in psycho-
pathological disruptions, independently or interdependently. The hor-
rifying experience of "falling to pieces" gets hold of the person. To the
degree in which this happens, one's world also falls to pieces. It ceases
to be a world, in the sense of a meaningful whole. Things no longer speak
to man; they lose their power to enter into a meaningful encounter with
man, because man himself has lost this power. In extreme cases the
complete unreality of one's world is felt; nothing is left except the
awareness of one's own empty self.[42]

In short, on the first level of the ontological structure, estrangement takes
the form of the disintegration of the centered self and the reduction of the
self's world to a mere environment.

On the second level of the structure, estrangement consists in the destruction of the essential polar relationship of the ontological elements.[43]
Freedom becomes arbitrariness, destiny becomes mechanical necessity.
Dynamics degenerates into a formless urge for self-transcendence, form
degenerates into external law. Individualization is cut off from universality so that one is shut within oneself at the same time that one falls under
the power of objects; by swallowing the empty shell of subjectivity, those
objects in turn change one into a mere object as well.

It will be recalled that the third level of the ontological structure concerns the characteristics of being that make the transition from essence to
existence a possibility. The state of estrangement or "fallenness" goes beyond formal possibility to actuality: the transition takes place.

As for estrangement on the fourth level of the structure, the categories of finite being and thinking, Tillich explains that

the function of the categories of finitude is changed under the conditions of existence. In the categories, the unity of being and nonbeing in
all finite beings is manifest. Therefore, they produce anxiety; but they
can be affirmed by courage, if the predominance of being over non-being
is experienced. In the state of estrangement, the relation to the ultimate

---

[42]*ST*, 2:61.

[43]See ibid., 62-66.

power of being is lost. In that state, the categories control existence and produce a double reaction toward them—resistance and despair.[44]

One attempts to resist the ultimate threat of nonbeing present in the categories under the conditions of existential estrangement, but such resistance must be unsuccessful, because in the state of estrangement, one is cut off from being-itself as the power of being. Despair results.

Despair is a mood providing an awareness not just of existential distortion of the categories but of existential distortion in general. As Tillich, influenced by Kierkegaard's *The Sickness Unto Death*, describes it:

> Despair is the state of inescapable conflict. It is the conflict, on the one hand, between what one potentially is and therefore ought to be and, on the other hand, what one actually is in the combination of freedom and destiny. The pain of despair is the agony of being responsible for the loss of the meaning of one's existence and of being unable to recover it. One is shut up in one's self and in the conflict with one's self. One cannot escape, because one cannot escape from one's self.[45]

Tillich points out that the inability to escape from the dilemma of existential distortion is expressed in the traditional theological metaphor "the bondage of the will."[46]

The empowerment effected by the biblical symbol of Jesus as the Christ can be described this way: the symbol of the Christ overcomes the conflict between one's desire to be the sort of being one essentially ought to be and one's inability to attain that essential being. Within the ontological structure, this conflict, manifest in the mood of despair, takes the form of the distortion of that structure. The power of New Being communicated by the symbol of the Christ, as a power transcending the poles of the structure and grounding them in their essential "depth," is the power of being-it-

---

[44]Ibid., 68.

[45]Ibid., 75.

[46]See ibid., 78-80.

self.[47] The symbol of the Christ can therefore be correlated with the question of how it is possible to overcome existential estrangement, and the symbol can be located by saying that it provides a dialectical awareness of being-itself from the perspective of the ontological structure qua "*structure of destruction.*"[48]

The indirect interpretation of the symbol of the Christ provided by the hermeneutical correlation sharply contrasts with any attempted interpretation of it provided by a literal description of its contents. What is to be made, then, of the early church's attempt to interpret the christological symbols through concepts drawn from Greek philosophy? If that undertaking was meant to exhaust the meaning of Jesus as the Christ in literal terms, it must be judged misguided.[49] But the undertaking can be seen instead as meant to protect the meaning of the symbols.[50]

For example, the Chalcedonian dogma can be understood, in Tillichian terms, as having protected the symbol of the Christ from the heresy—called Docetism—suggesting that New Being cannot be present under the conditions of actual existence. Such interpretation can be seen, furthermore, as protecting symbols against crude literalistic distortion. Tillich's comments on "demythologization" are of interest here.

> "Demythologization" can mean two things, and the failure to distinguish between them has led to the confusion which characterizes the discussion. It can mean the fight against the literalistic distortion of symbols and myths. . . . But demythologization can also mean the re-

---

[47]Evidently, Tillich thinks of being-itself's overcoming of estrangement (New Being) primarily in terms of the actual transformation of distorted being, but he indicates that one moment of the empowerment involved in New Being consists of the power to overcome despair by "accepting the fact that one is accepted" by being-itself. That is, there is an element here equivalent to the Lutheran, forensic view of justification by grace (though Tillich expresses some reservations about the term *forensic*), in addition to the more Augustinian element. See *ST*, 2:176-80. Compare *The Courage to Be*, 171-90.

[48]See *ST*, 2:60.

[49]See ibid., 140, 142.

[50]See ibid., 138-50.

moval of myth as a vehicle of religious expression and the substitution of science and morals. In this sense demythologization must be strongly rejected. It would deprive religion of its language; it would silence the experience of the holy. Symbols and myths cannot be criticized simply because they are symbols. They must be criticized on the basis of their power to express what they are supposed to express, namely, in this instance, the New Being in Jesus as the Christ.[51]

Only if the christological dogmas of the church avoid demythologization in the latter sense can they be considered legitimate.

The material that makes up the symbol of the Christ must have affinities with being-itself as the power of New Being. The New Testament picture of Jesus as the Christ, interpreted here as a symbol, is itself made up of stories and symbols. Tillich maintains that this picture is nonetheless a unity, that there is an underlying substance, which all the various stories and symbols contribute to and none contradict. This unifying substance of the picture of the Christ

> shines through as the power of the New Being in a three-fold color: first and decisively, as the undisrupted unity of the center of his being with God; second, as the serenity and majesty of him who preserves this unity against all the attacks coming from estranged existence; and, third, as the self-transcending love which represents and actualizes the divine love in taking the existential self-destruction upon itself. There is no passage in the Gospels—or, for that matter, in the Epistles—which takes away the power of this three-fold manifestation of the New Being in the biblical picture of Jesus as the Christ.[52]

Tillich sums up this unity in his description of the picture of the Christ as "the picture of a personal life which is subjected to all the consequences of existential estrangement but wherein estrangement is conquered in himself and a permanent unity is kept with God."[53] The affinities this picture shares with being-itself (being-itself being that which can overcome estrangement) are thus obvious, for the picture describes the concrete ef-

---

[51]Ibid., 152.

[52]Ibid., 138.

[53]Ibid., 135.

fects of being-itself occurring within the structure of finite being as "fallen" being.[54]

Life and the Spirit

While the first major part of Tillich's system is concerned with essential being and the second with existential or "fallen" being, the third major part deals with what Tillich terms "life." One way Tillich defines life is as an ambiguous mixture of essential and existential elements.[55] He asserts that "essential as well as existential elements are always abstractions from the concrete actuality of being, namely, 'Life.' "[56] To say that essence and existence are abstractions is not to say that the analyses Tillich performs in the first two major parts of the system do not apply to reality as it is actually experienced. Indeed, it has been shown how two symbols that belong in the context of the structure of being qua essential structure and

---

[54]It has been pointed out that the biblical picture of the Christ is a response to a historical occurrence, an occurrence that Tillich believes was the decisive entrance of New Being into human existence. The empowering quality of the picture guarantees the reality of the historical occurrence (though not all the details of that occurrence as reported in the New Testament [see *ST*, 114-15]), and Tillich claims that characteristics of that occurrence can be singled out as necessary conditions for its having been the decisive manifestation of New Being. For instance, the New Being, if it was to conquer estrangement, had to appear in a *personal* life (see *ST*, 2:98, 120) and at the same time had to have *universal* significance (see *ST*, 2:150-65). What, then, is the relationship between the symbolic picture of the Christ and the historical fact it is based on? If the symbol's power guarantees the reality of the historical occurrence, it would seem that the picture is dependent for its power upon that original occurrence, a dependence Tillich might explain as being fulfilled by saying that the actual historical person who was the bearer of New Being had first to conquer estrangement "in principle" (see *ST*, 2:98) so that the picture of the Christ could subsequently empower those who were confronted by it. As a result, is one to conclude that the picture is only effective as a source of New Being because its symbolic material depicts a *personal* life that has *universal* significance (Jesus of Nazareth as the incarnation of God)?

[55]See *ST*, 3:12.

[56]*ST*, 2:28.

in the structure of being qua structure of destruction, respectively, play important roles as sources of empowerment. In what sense, then, are essence and existence abstractions while life is a concrete reality? Apparently, while the essential character of the structure of being does have concrete implications for human experience—one must always courageously affirm one's being over against the threat of nonbeing—and while the character of the structure as subject to existential distortion concretely affects one's life—one must always seek that which will conquer estrangement—human experience can never be described purely in terms of essence or purely in terms of existence. Essential and existential elements are mixed together in human experience.

But Tillich's analysis of life does not consist simply of adding together essential and existential elements. Note that the previous quotation refers to life as the "actuality of being." In other words, life is to be defined as the actualization of potential being.[57] Tillich's discussion of life focuses on the dynamic element in being, the movement from potential to actual.[58] By concentrating on this dynamic element, Tillich uncovers not only a mixture of essence and existence but also an aspect of the ontological structure not evident in the previous parts of his investigation.

> Life was defined as the actualization of potential being. In every life process such actualization takes place. The terms "act," "action," "actual," denote a centrally intended movement ahead, a going-out from a center of action. But this going-out takes place in such a way that the center is not lost in the outgoing movement. The self-identity remains in the self-alteration. The other (*alterum*) in the process of alteration is turned both away from the center and back toward it. So we can distinguish three elements in the process of life: self-identity, self-altera-

---

[57]Tillich terms this "the ontological concept of life." See *ST*, 3:11.

[58]It might be suggested that, since existence as the transition from essential being to "fallen" being already involves the actualization of potential being, the attempt to distinguish life from existence by defining life as actualized being must fail. This is the position taken by Adrian Thatcher in *The Ontology of Paul Tillich* (Oxford: Oxford University Press, 1978) 153-57. But it could be said that while Tillich's analysis of existence concentrates on the result of actualization in the structure of being, his analysis of life concentrates on the movement of actualization.

tion, and return to one's self. Potentiality becomes actuality only through these three elements in the process which we call life.[59]

Tillich then describes what he calls the three "functions" of life:

> self-integration under the principle of centeredness, self-creation under the principle of growth, and self-transcendence under the principle of sublimity. The basic structure of self-identity and self-alteration is effective in each, and each is dependent on the basic polarities of being: self-integration on the polarity of individualization and participation, self-creation on the polarity of dynamics and form, self-transcendence on the polarity of freedom and destiny. And the structure of self-identity and self-alteration is rooted in the basic ontological self-world correlation.[60]

Thus, when Tillich describes life as an ambiguous mixture of essential and existential elements, he is not simply adding together the data adduced in the two previous parts of the system, which deal with essence and existence respectively, but building upon what his analysis of life as the actualization of being has revealed.

> The three functions of life unite elements of self-identity with elements of self-alteration. But this unity is threatened by existential estrangement, which drives life in one or the other direction, thus disrupting the unity. To the degree in which this disruption is real, self-integration is countered by disintegration, self-creation is countered by destruction, self-transcendence is countered by profanization. Every life process has the ambiguity that the positive and negative elements are mixed in such a way that a definite separation of the negative from the positive is impossible: life at every moment is ambiguous.[61]

Evidently, then, the power required to overcome ambiguity, like the power required to enable courage and the power needed to conquer estrangement, must be being-itself as the ground of the structure of being and as its essential unity.

---

[59] *ST*, 3:30.

[60] Ibid., 32.

[61] Ibid., 32.

We can, says Tillich, distinguish different "dimensions" of life, with each succeeding dimension actualizing qualities contained only potentially in the preceding dimension. Tillich treats five such dimensions: (1) the inorganic dimension, (2) the organic dimension, (3) the animal dimension or dimension of self-awareness, (4) the spiritual dimension, and (5) the dimension of history. Human self-consciousness is life in the dimension of spirit, a dimension Tillich describes as "the unity of life-power and life in meanings."[62] Spirit is to be understood as the unity of the ontological elements. Because the one side—including centered personality, self-transcending vitality, and freedom of self-determination—of each of the three sets of polarities can be summed up as power, and the other side—containing universal participation, forms and structures of reality, and limiting and directing destiny—can be summed up as meaning, spirit can be defined as the unity of power and meaning.[63] The precise characters of the three functions of life as they appear in the dimension of spirit are as follows: the self-integration of life in the dimension of spirit is morality, the self-creativity of life in the dimension of spirit is culture, and the self-transcendence of life in the dimension of spirit is religion.

The above description of life and spirit paves the way for the interpretation of the traditional Christian symbol of the divine Spirit. The term *Spirit* is used in Christianity to describe the presence of the divine within creaturely life. Thus, Tillich specifically designates the symbol of the Spirit as "Spiritual Presence."[64] The symbol of the Spiritual Presence empowers unambiguous life (though such unambiguous life is present only fragmentarily).[65] Therefore, the symbol of the Spiritual Presence can be correlated with the quest for unambiguous life and can be located by stating that it provides a dialectical awareness of being-itself from the perspective of the structure of being qua *structure of life*. Furthermore, the dimension of life involved is primarily the dimension of spirit.[66]

---

[62]Ibid., 22.

[63]See *ST*, 1:249-50.

[64]See *ST*, 3:107.

[65]See ibid., 138-41.

[66]See ibid., 107-108, 275-82. The two symbols Tillich discusses in the sec-

What affinities does the concept of spirit have with being-itself that would allow it to function as a symbol for being-itself in this context? For human being, the dynamic of life is a matter of spirit. Thus, the depth of that dynamic, being-itself as the dynamic of life's ground, can be symbolized as Spirit, the presence of the Divine Spirit within the realm of human spirit. As the etymology of the word suggests, the concept of spirit is well suited to symbolize the presence of being-itself *within* human life: the spirit is the breath within the body that animates the body and gives it life. This sense of Spirit as Spiritual Presence is expressed, for instance, in the apostle Paul's notion of "the Spirit himself bearing witness with our spirit that we are children of God."[67]

Interestingly, with regard to the three major parts of the *Systematic Theology*, Tillich's decision to concentrate upon the symbols of God, the Christ, and the Spiritual Presence is an obvious reflection of the Christian doctrine of the trinitarian nature of God. The recognition that each of these three symbols accomplishes a particular sort of empowerment aids in understanding why the notion of the Trinity arose. This threefold symbolism is not merely an accidental grouping but arises, at least in part, according to Tillich's analysis, from human being's search for a threefold deliverance or empowerment.[68]

---

tion of his system entitled "History and the Kingdom of God," a section separated from "Life and the Spirit" for practical reasons, can be located near the symbol of Spiritual Presence. "The three symbols for unambiguous life mutually include each other, but because of the different symbolic material they use, it is preferable to apply them in different directions of meaning: Spiritual Presence for the conquest of the ambiguities of life under the dimension of the spirit, Kingdom of God for the conquest of the ambiguities of life under the dimension of history, and Eternal Life for the conquest of the ambiguities of life beyond history" (*ST*, 3:109). As for revelation, the other topic treated separately from the three main parts of the *Systematic Theology*: each of the empowering symbols treated by Tillich is a revealing symbol, for the presence to consciousness of being-itself entails that reason has been opened to its "depth," that is, to revelation.

[67]Rom. 8:16, Revised Standard Version.

[68]Compare *ST*, 3:283-86.

The Hermeneutical Correlation
and the Secondary Literature

Widespread interest among theologians in the methodical character of Tillich's thought has resulted in a secondary literature on the method of correlation rivaling in size the secondary literature on Tillich's doctrine of religious symbols. An explicit distinction between what I have termed the apologetic and the hermeneutical correlations is not apparent in that literature. That this distinction is missing is unsurprising: Tillich himself never makes that distinction explicitly; I have claimed that it is an important implicit distinction in his system.

This is not to say, however, that the secondary literature is irrelevant with respect to this topic. While most treatments of the method of correlation deal only with the apologetic correlation—because it is the one illuminated by Tillich's own comments on the purpose of his method—there are some discussions of Tillich in the literature at least indirectly relevant to my notion of the hermeneutical version of correlation. Those discussions can be divided into two basic categories. The first category contains those books and articles that, by uncovering the ontological-structural relationship on which Tillich's hermeneutical correlation of philosophy and religion is based, lay the groundwork for a recognition of the hermeneutical correlation. The second category contains a kind of critique of Tillich's method of correlation that, because its formulators think exclusively in terms of the apologetic correlation, needs to be confronted with the hermeneutical correlation. This confrontation is further necessitated by the ubiquity of the critique; one sometimes gets the impression that it represents an almost unanimous judgment upon Tillich's method.

At the center of the hermeneutical correlation lies the juxtaposition of philosophical questions with religious answers to form descriptions of the structure of finite being over against being-itself as the ground or depth of that structure. The apologetic correlation, on the other hand, understands the philosophical questions as representing a particular, contingent cultural situation. When the symbols representing being-itself are correlated with these questions, one finds answers to the needs of a special group rather than finding the kind of ontological-structural relationship upon which the hermeneutical correlation is built. While most commentators and critics have overlooked this ontological-structural relationship, a number of important works have brought it to light. Perhaps the earliest of these is Bernard Loomer's 1956 article entitled, simply enough, "Tillich's Theology of Correlation." There Loomer explains that

> philosophy's major preoccupation is with the structure of being or the categorial structure of reality. Theology's main business is with the depth or the ground of the structure of being. The questions that philosophy asks derive from an analysis of the structure of being as this is found under the conditions of existence. Philosophy cannot adequately answer the problems derived from its own analysis of the structure of being as found in existence, because existence itself is the problem. . . . The incompleteness of existence can be answered only by that which lies beyond existence, by that which includes, but is not bound by, the structure of being. This is being itself, the ground of being, found as a depth within the structure of being. This depth is disclosed in revelation, wherein the unconditional reveals itself through the transparency of something finite. An adequate answer to, or a resource for, man's ultimate questions cannot come from structure but only from a depth of being which includes, but is more than, structure.[69]

Aside from using the word *theology* where one perhaps should speak of *religion*,[70] Loomer describes clearly the ontological-structural relationship contained within the method of correlation that makes the hermeneutical method of correlation possible. Loomer sees, furthermore, a connection between Tillich's notion of correlation and his earlier ontological-structural account of the relation between religion and culture as one of substance (*Gehalt*) and form.

> One of Tillich's basic formulas is that religion is the substance of culture and that culture is the form of religion. Religion and culture are not separate realms. They are mutually implicative. Religion is con-

---

[69]Bernard Loomer, "Tillich's Theology of Correlation," *Journal of Religion* 36 (May 1956): 151.

[70]See Scharlemann's formulation, quoted in the introduction to this chapter.

cerned with the depth within culture, while culture is the structure of being in existence in terms of which the depth takes on form.[71]

In other words, Loomer shows that behind the discussion in the *Systematic Theology* of correlation as a juxtaposition of a particular cultural situation and Christian symbols (the apologetic correlation) there lies Tillich's earlier work on the form-*Gehalt* relationship between culture and being-itself. This connection in turn makes the existence of the hermeneutical correlation alongside the apologetic more apparent.

The most thorough exposition of the formal, structural relationship between the correlative elements in Tillich's system is to be found in Robert P. Scharlemann's *Reflection and Doubt in the Thought of Paul Tillich*.[72] Discussing the self-world structure of being—Scharlemann speaks of the "subjectival" and the "objectival" poles presupposed in one's thinking anything at all[73]—the author explains that

> in critical reflection I endeavor to grasp the objectivity of whatever I am dealing with in thought; I endeavor to understand what it is. By contrast, in doubting response I reply to the power (the subjectivity) acting upon me. Critical reflection endeavors to grasp the objectivity of the objectival, and doubting response replies to its subjectivity.[74]

From this perspective, founded upon an interest in the ontological-structural characteristic of Tillich's system, Scharlemann can survey dimensions of that system: "Self, World, God," "Subjectivity and Objectivity in the Objectival," "Subject and Subject," "Structure and Depth," "Question and Answer."[75] Because the question-answer relationship is most explicit in Tillich's thought, Scharlemann indicates how those other aspects of Tillich's thinking he uncovers are connected to that relationship:

---

[71]Loomer, "Tillich's Theology of Correlation," 153.

[72]Scharlemann's formulation of the relationship between philosophy, religion, and theology in his "Tillich's Method of Correlation: Two Proposed Revisions" was mentioned earlier.

[73]See Scharlemann, *Reflection and Doubt in the Thought of Paul Tillich,* x-xi.

[74]Ibid., xi.

[75]These are the titles of chapters 2, 3, 4, 5, and 6 respectively.

> Questioning is a basic form of critical reflection; receiving answers is a
> basic form of distancing response; existential questions and religious
> answers are movements in which the subject-object structure is opened
> to its depth, in one case as abyss, in the other as ground; in both cases
> all elements of subjectivity and objectivity are involved. The correlation
> of questions and answers is, therefore, a recapitulation of the problems
> of reflection and response, subjectivity and objectivity.[76]

Furthermore, Scharlemann connects Tillich's earlier work on the formal
structural relationship between religion and culture with the *Systematic
Theology*.[77]

That recognition of an ontological-structural relationship in Tillich's
method of correlation via a grasp of the tie between his earlier work on
culture and religion with the *Systematic Theology*, which is a dimension
of both Loomer's and Scharlemann's analyses, also appears in other writers. Jay M. van Hook, in his doctoral dissertation on "Paul Tillich's Conception of the Relation between Philosophy and Theology," concludes of
the *Systematic Theology*:

> Tillich's distinction between philosophy and theology remains puzzling
> . . . until it is realized that the presupposition of the relation between
> philosophy and theology is his view of the relation between *form* and
> *content*. On the basis of this presupposition, Tillich's view may be stated
> thus: philosophy is the form of theology, and theology is the content or
> substance of philosophy.[78]

That is, in the *Systematic Theology* the relationship between philosophy
and theology is based upon the form-content relationship between culture
and religion laid out in Tillich's earlier works. While Tillich himself never
makes this connection explicit, van Hook notes that "philosophy is clearly
a cultural activity" in the *Systematic Theology*.[79] Van Hook's exposition

---

[76]Ibid., 138.

[77]See ibid., 22-59, 113-35, and "The Scope of Systematics: An Analysis of
Tillich's Two Systems," *Journal of Religion* 48 (April 1968): 136-49.

[78]Jay M. van Hook, "Paul Tillich's Conception of the Relation between Philosophy and Theology" (Ph.D. diss., Columbia University, 1966) 142.

[79]Ibid., 145.

would have been improved if he had observed that distinction between religion and theology mentioned here several times. Even in the *Systematic Theology*, it is not *theology* that is the content or *Gehalt* of philosophy, but *religion*.

John P. Clayton, too, notices that Tillich carries the form-content pattern of his earlier works on culture into his method of correlation. In *The Concept of Correlation: Paul Tillich and the Possibility of a Mediating Theology*, Clayton speaks of questioning and answering, and form and content, as "two models of a correlative relation."[80] But Clayton points out that, while Tillich's form-content pattern does indeed carry into his method of correlation, its character is somewhat altered. Whereas earlier, Tillich emphasizes the unity of form and content—that is, cultural structure and religious ground or *Gehalt*—with regard to the method of correlation, he emphasizes the existential estrangement of cultural form and religious content.[81]

This estrangement is what necessitates the correlation of the two. Nevertheless, Clayton's account still clarifies the formal, structural relationship in the *Systematic Theology* that makes the hermeneutical correlation possible. Furthermore, Clayton provides a thorough analysis of the development of the form-content model in Tillich's work.[82]

Having considered those works in which the author pays special attention to the ontological-structural relationship between the elements of Tillich's method of correlation, one can turn to three articles that at least suggest that relationship. In his analysis of "The Conceptual Structure of Tillich's Method of Correlation," Douglass Lewis complains that Tillich is involved in a contradiction: on the one hand, Tillich claims that philosophy and theology are logically distinct, but, on the other hand, he says that theology can answer questions posed by philosophy. Lewis holds that questions that operate according to one sort of logic cannot be answered out of a different logical context; questions from within one "language game" (in the Wittgensteinian sense) cannot receive answers from another "language game."

----

[80]Clayton, *The Concept of Correlation*, 153ff.

[81]See ibid., 221.

[82]See ibid., 191-222.

What Tillich actually does, contrary to what he says, is reduce theology to ontology. That is, according to Lewis, the concepts Tillich categorizes under "theology" have their meaning and use determined by ontology. Then Lewis acknowledges that religious symbols, as opposed to the theological concepts used to interpret them, are independent of ontology. In order to explain this independence, he refers to Scharlemann's formulation: "Religious assertions are symbolic (referring to the depth of being), ontological assertions are literal (referring to the structure of being), and theological assertions are literal descriptions of the correlation between the religious symbols and the ontological concepts."[83] Thus, Lewis's article is worth citing (even though it is dependent upon Scharlemann for this insight into the structure of correlation).

Noriyoshi Tamaru also briefly indicates the formal, structural relationship that makes the hermeneutical correlation possible, and he does so in language that points to the connection between Tillich's early work on form and *Gehalt* and the later method of correlation:

> Wie wir verfolgt haben, handelt es sich bei der 'Korrelation' um das Aufeinanderbeziehen von dem religiösen Gehalt, der in der biblischen Botschaft enthalten ist, und den begrifflichen Formen, die durch eine philosophische Analyse des menschlichen Daseins einer Zeit gewonnen werden müssen.[84]

It is unfortunate that Tamaru does not develop his insight more fully.

A third example of a brief, undeveloped account of the ontological-structural relationship at work in Tillich's correlation is Langdon Gilkey's "Tillich: The Master of Mediation." Gilkey recognizes that philosophy's role is the analysis of the structure of being and that that structure must be contrasted with the "depth" of being.[85] And Gilkey is able to relate the early Tillich to the late on this topic:

---

[83]Quoted by Douglass Lewis, "The Conceptual Structure of Tillich's Method of Correlation," *Encounter* 28 (1967): 273 n.38.

[84]Noriyoshi Tamaru, "Motiv und Struktur der Theologie Paul Tillichs," *Neue Zeitschrift für systematische Theologie und Religionsphilosophie* 3 (1961): 8.

[85]See Gilkey, "Tillich: The Master of Mediation," in *The Theology of Paul Tillich*, 38.

Culture lives from its religious substance, from the manifestation of the
ground, power and meaning of being that establishes that culture's life.
Correspondingly, philosophy, as the epitome of cultural reason, lives
from its relation with its own depth via that cultural *gestalt* or religious
substance. Every great epoch of philosophy expresses and so lives from
the religious substance of its culture insofar as it depends as a condition
for its own possibility on the unity of thought and being, subject and
object, of reality and value, apprehended in that culture's creative life.

With this understanding of the relation of culture and the religious, Tillich's insistence that "religion provides the answers to philosophy's questions" makes sense.[86]

There is a link between the form-content pattern of the early work on religion and culture, and the method of correlation found in the *Systematic
Theology*.

Finally, there is a small group of relatively recent articles in the German literature on Tillich that does deal with the ontological-structural
presuppositions of the method of correlation. These articles are not as useful in uncovering the foundation of the hermeneutical correlation, however, because they are in effect critiques of Tillich's ontology. That is, they
claim that the ontology Tillich employs is different from what Tillich himself recognizes it to be, or that it involves difficulties that he does not ac-
knowledge, while it has been suggested here that the hermeneutical
correlation is implied in a reading of Tillich's system consistent with Tillich's own account of that system. Martin Repp, for example, claims that
the background of Tillich's method of correlation is Hegel's idealism, that
it is a three-stage deductive dialectic moving from concept, through existential problem, to answer.[87] In this same category might be placed articles
by Peter Schwanz[88] and Joachim Ringleben.[89]

---

[86]Ibid., 40.

[87]Martin Repp, "Zum Hintergrund von Paul Tillichs Korrelations-Methode," *Neue Zeitschrift für systematische Theologie und Religionsphilosophie* 24
(1982): 206-18.

[88]See Peter Schwanz, "Das für Tillichs Methode der Korrelation grundlegende Problem der Vermittlung," *Neue Zeitschrift für systematische Theologie
und Religionsphilosophie* 15 (1973): 254-71 and "Ontologie oder transzenden-

One can move now from those books and articles recognizing the ontological-structural relationship involved in correlation to those containing a particular kind of critique of Tillich's method of correlation. This critique can be profitably confronted with the implications of the hermeneutical correlation because it is a critique that seems to think exclusively in terms of the apologetic version of correlation.

When he describes the method of correlation in volume 2 of the *Systematic Theology*, Tillich claims that the relation of the questions to the answers can be described both in terms of independence and of interdependence. On the one hand, one cannot derive the answers from the questions nor the questions from the answers:

> The existential question, namely, man himself in the conflicts of his existential situation, is not the source for the revelatory answer formulated by theology. One cannot derive the divine self-manifestation from an analysis of the human predicament. God speaks to the human situation, against it, and for it. Theological supranaturalism, as represented, for example, by contemporary neo-orthodox theology, is right in asserting the inability of man to reach God under his own power. Man is the question, not the answer. It is equally wrong to derive the question implied in human existence from the revelatory answer. This is impossible because the revelatory answer is meaningless if there is no question to which it is the answer. Man cannot receive an answer to a question he has not asked.[90]

But, on the other hand, there is also an element of interdependence:

> While the material of the existential question is the very expression of the human predicament, the form of the question is determined by the total system and by the answers given in it. The question implied in human finitude is directed toward the answer: the eternal. . . . The other side of the correlation is the influence of the existential questions on the theological answers. . . . The form of the theological answer is *not* in-

---

taler Relationalismus? Die Fragwürdigkeit der Ontologie Tillichs," *Theologische Zeitschrift* 29 (1973): 419-27.

[89]See Joachim Ringleben, "Paul Tillichs Theologie der Methode," *Neue Zeitschrift für systematische Theologie und Religionsphilosophie* 17 (1975): 246-68.

[90]*ST*, 2:13.

dependent of the form of the existential question. If theology gives the answer, "the Christ," to the question implied in human estrangement, it does so differently, depending on whether the reference is to the existential conflicts of Jewish legalism, to the existential despair of Greek skepticism, or to the threat of nihilism as expressed in twentieth-century literature, art and philosophy.[91]

In short, the *substance* of the question is independent of the substance of the answer and vice versa, but both question and answer can influence the *form* of their counterparts.[92]

Many critics have contended, however, that the method of correlation, by its very nature, violates the independence of the substance of the question or of the substance of the answer. Unsurprisingly, theological commentators, by and large, have been more worried about the threat to the substance of the religious answers. The most frequently cited of those who express this concern is Kenneth Hamilton. Hamilton charges that "since the correlation of 'situation' and 'message' turns out to be a reading of the religious 'message' wholly in terms of a philosophical analysis of the 'situation,' Tillich's method cannot be other than a *reduction* of Christian doctrine to make it agree with his ontology."[93] Hamilton points to page 64 of volume 1 of the *Systematic Theology* as evidence for his contention, where he quotes Tillich as saying,

> God is the answer to the question implied in human finitude. This answer cannot be derived from the analysis of existence. However, if the notion of God appears in systematic correlation with the threat of non-being which is implied in existence, God must be called the infinite power of being which resists the threat of non-being. In classical theology this is being-itself.[94]

---

[91]Ibid., 15-16.

[92]"Substance" is Tillich's own word. See *ST*, 2:15.

[93]Kenneth Hamilton, "Tillich's Method of Correlation," *Canadian Journal of Theology* 5 (April 1959): 91.

[94]Quoted in ibid., 91-92. The same reference is found in Hamilton's *The System and the Gospel: A Critique of Paul Tillich* (New York: Macmillan, 1963) 122-23, the sixth chapter of which is devoted to the method of correlation. In

In his well-known book on Tillich, *The System and the Gospel*, Hamilton sees himself playing a role over against Tillich's theological method analogous to that taken by Kierkegaard vis-à-vis Hegel's system.

One could hardly expect Karl Barth to remain silent on this issue and indeed he does not:

> Since Tillich's theological answers are not only taken from the Bible, but with equal emphasis from church history, the history of culture generally, and the history of religion—and above all, since their meaning and placement is dependent upon their relation to philosophical questions—could not these answers be taken as philosophy just as well (or better than?) they could be taken as theology? Will these theological answers allow themselves to be pressed into this scheme without suffering harm to what in any case is their biblical content? Is man with his philosophical questions, for Tillich, not more than simply the beginning point of the development of this whole method of correlation? Is he not, in that he himself knows which questions to ask, anticipating their correctness, and therefore already in possession of the answers and their consequences?[95]

Barth's statement appears as an introduction to Alexander McKelway's *Systematic Theology of Paul Tillich*, a work that elaborates this basic Barthian viewpoint.

One finds in the literature on Tillich a series of subtle variations on the position exemplified by the quotations from Hamilton and Barth. Erwin Reisner, thinking not just of Tillich but about the general strategy of juxtaposing philosophical questions and theological answers, complains that so long as one understands the sought-after theological answer as a direct answer to *one's own question*, one is standing on the ground of a pre-Christian religiousness, on the ground of the Apostle Thomas, who

---

both cases, Hamilton misquotes Tillich slightly: Tillich speaks of the notion of God appearing "in systematic theology in correlation with the threat of nonbeing," not of that notion appearing "in systematic correlation with the threat of non-being."

[95]Karl Barth, "An Introductory Report," in Alexander McKelway, *The Systematic Theology of Paul Tillich: A Review and Analysis* (Richmond: John Knox, 1964) 13.

would only believe after he saw.[96] Josef Schmitz wonders about the possible danger of the method of correlation: the existential question might be thought to exhaust the content of revelation. Couldn't revelation perhaps communicate more than what questions derived from human existence ask about?[97] Klaus-Dieter Nörenberg suggests that the figurative quality of religious symbols, as Tillich understands it, corresponds to the existential questions with which those symbols are correlated. That is, through its figurative quality the symbol as answer corresponds to the question. But if so, the religious answer is determined and defined anthropologically.[98] According to George F. Thomas, Tillich ought to allow for a Christian perspective in formulating his philosophical questions as well as his religious answers, for the lack of a fully Christian analysis of the human situation threatens to pervert the answers.[99] Robert C. Johnson takes a similar approach, arguing that a non-Christian analysis of the human situation leads to a false understanding of the problem in which human beings find themselves; Tillich's philosophical account of estrangement does not do justice to the biblical description of sin as active rebellion. This lack in turn affects the answers: there is, for example, too little emphasis on forgiveness and atonement in Tillich's system.[100] Gunda Schneider-Flume also worries that Tillich's philosophical analysis perverts the understanding of sin.[101]

All of these writers fear that Tillich's method of correlation undermines the truth of the Christian message. They would say that the philo-

---

[96]See Erwin Reisner, "Die Frage der Philosophie und die Antwort der Theologie," *Zeitschrift für Theologie und Kirche* 53 (1956): 251-63.

[97]See Schmitz, *Die apologetische Theologie Paul Tillichs,* 271-80.

[98]See Nörenberg, *Analogia Imaginis,* 219-28.

[99]See George F. Thomas, "The Method and Structure of Tillich's Theology," in *The Theology of Paul Tillich,* 2d ed., 135-39.

[100]See Robert C. Johnson, *Authority in Protestant Theology* (Philadelphia: Westminster, 1959) 118-24.

[101]See Gunda Schneider-Flume, " 'Entsprechungsdenken' und Sündenerkenntnis. Die Auswirkung der Methode der Korrelation auf das Sündenverständnis in der systematischen Theologie Paul Tillichs," *Zeitschrift für Theologie und Kirche* 76 (1979): 489-513.

sophical questions affect not only the form of the religious answers but their substance as well.[102]

There are those, however, who see the opposite defect in Tillich's method of correlation. They believe that the religious answers tend to determine the content of the philosophical questions. Harvey Cox, a representative of the so-called secular theology of a few decades past, holds that Tillich's philosophical questions fail to represent the current cultural situation even though that is their appointed task. Tillich's philosophical analysis of the contemporary situation is colored by his own theological orientation. Thus, his questions are not those asked by modern secular persons. They are questions that arise out of his mourning over the death of God, while secular persons never depended upon that God in the first place.[103]

Similarly, Edward Schillebeeckx claims that the question-answer relationship presupposes that the questions and the answers operate within the context of the same "language game." Tillich seems to be aware of this problem, according to Schillebeeckx, so he formulates the philosophical questions anew in light of the Christian answers. He turns his philosophical questions into theological or Christian questions. But this reformulation short-circuits the purpose of correlation, for the answers to such reformulated questions are valid only for Christians, not for human beings universally.[104]

---

[102]See also Hendrik Kraemer, "A Criticism of Paul Tillich's 'Reconciliation,' " in *Religion and the Christian Faith* (Philadelphia: Westminster, 1956) 426-48; John B. Cobb, *Living Options in Protestant Theology: A Survey of Methods* (Philadelphia: Westminster, 1962) 276-83; Michael Palmer, "Correlation and Ontology: A Study in Tillich's Christology," *Downside Review* 96 (1978): 120-31.

[103]See Harvey Cox, *The Secular City* (New York: Macmillan, 1965) 78-81.

[104]See Edward Schillebeeckx, "Correlation between Human Question and Christian Answer," in *The Understanding of Faith,* trans. N. D. Smith (New York: Seabury, 1974) 78-101. Douglass Lewis's "The Conceptual Structure of Tillich's Method of Correlation," which also contained the Wittgenstein-inspired claim that Tillich's questions and answers must be derived from the same language game if they are to correspond to one another, was mentioned above. But note that Lewis and Schillebeeckx come to opposite conclusions about which language game Tillich chooses, the philosophical-ontological or the religious.

According to David Tracy, Tillich's version of correlation does not take the philosophical-analysis side of the correlation seriously enough, for it is allowed to generate only the *questions.* Why should not one also consider the *answers* made available by the philosophical movements—existentialism, for example—from which Tillich borrows?[105]

Wilhelm Weischedel asserts that what Tillich calls ontology is not really a purely philosophical analysis of being but is in fact theological: "Der hier auftauchende Seinsbegriff ist ersichtlich nicht ontologischen, sondern soteriologischen Ursprungs; er betrifft Heil und Unheil des Menschen."[106] It seems that the Christian, religious answer has determined the very substance of the philosophical side of the correlation.[107]

As if to cover all the bases, there are also those critics who embrace a third option. They hold that the method of correlation Tillich employs threatens the substance of both philosophy and religion simultaneously. Thus, Thomas J. J. Altizer states that Tillich's method results in philosophical questions that do not represent true contemporary *Existenz* and religious answers not based upon a genuine biblical, eschatological transcendence.[108] According to Gordon Kaufman, "philosophy and theology constantly tend to absorb each other" in Tillich's system.[109] Much the same

---

[105]See David Tracy, *Blessed Rage for Order* (New York: Seabury, 1975) 45-46.

[106]Wilhelm Weischedel, "Paul Tillich's philosophische Theologie: Ein eherbietiger Widerspruch," in *Der Spannungsbogen: Festgabe für Paul Tillich zum 75. Geburtstag,* ed. Karl Hennig (Stuttgart: Evangelisches Verlagswerk, 1961) 36.

[107]See also Heinz Zahrnt, *The Question of God: Protestant Theology in the Twentieth Century,* trans. R. A. Wilson (New York: Harcourt Brace Jovanovich, 1969) 319, 321, 334-35; von Kriegstein, *Paul Tillichs Methode der Korrelation und Symbolbegriff,* 57-68.

[108]See Thomas J. J. Altizer and William Hamilton, *Radical Theology and the Death of God* (Indianapolis: Bobbs-Merrill, 1966) 10-11, 105-109.

[109]Gordon D. Kaufman, "Can a Man Serve Two Masters?" *Theology Today* 15 (April 1958): 63.

point is made by other writers, among them Bernard Martin, John Morris, and George Tavard.[110]

If all the critics dealt with thus far fear that Tillich's method violates the independent substance of either or both of the two poles of correlation, John Clayton fears otherwise. In *The Concept of Correlation*, mentioned earlier, Clayton holds that Tillich violates the principle of interdependence. Clayton is concerned with the creation of a theology that can effect a mediation between Christian faith and contemporary culture, and he suggests that any theology that is to succeed at this task must solve what he calls "Schleiermacher's dilemma": the relationship between Christian faith and the larger culture in which it finds itself must be such that the autonomy or independent structure of neither is threatened, while at the same time both stand in reciprocal relation to one another, each influencing the other.[111]

Clayton judges that Tillich fails to solve Schleiermacher's dilemma. Tillich's failure, according to Clayton, is due to the manner in which he uses the two models of a correlative relationship with which, as noted above, Clayton chooses to deal.

> On its own the question-answer model fails to satisfy the autonomy condition; on its own, the form-content model fails to satisfy the reciprocity condition; the particular way they are combined by Tillich in his account of the method of correlation does not satisfy the reciprocity condition.[112]

The main problem seems to be that, because Tillich wants to protect the Christian message's autonomy, he assumes that it must in some sense possess an unchanging content and that, in Clayton's words, "*all instances of christian* [sic] *theology must have some property in common in virtue of*

---

[110]See Bernard Martin, *The Existentialist Theology of Paul Tillich* (New York: Bookman, 1963) 33-36; John Morris, "The Philosophical Basis of Tillich's Apologetic Theology," *Christian Scholar* 47 (Fall 1964): 233-42; George Tavard, "Paul Tillich's System," *Commonweal* 79 (7 February 1964): 566-68.

[111]See Clayton, *The Concept of Correlation*, 42.

[112]Ibid., 227.

which they are to be regarded as instances of christian theology."[113] This assumption, Clayton believes, stops Tillich from fulfilling the reciprocity condition necessary for a theology to mediate between Christianity and the larger culture, for it makes the Christian message, at least core elements of it, impervious to outside influence. Clayton suggests that, by understanding the Christian message's identity in terms of Wittgenstein's "family resemblance" rather than in terms of unchanging common properties possessed by all instances of that message and by the theology that articulates it, one could employ Tillich's method of correlation so as to satisfy both the autonomy condition and the reciprocity condition.[114]

This list of criticisms pertaining to the independence and interdependence of the two poles of Tillich's correlation operates within the context of what has been called here the apologetic correlation; the two poles are conceptualized as a cultural situation (pole 1) disclosed through philosophical analysis on the one side and the Christian message (pole 2) on the other. Expressed by someone like Kenneth Hamilton, the concern for the independence of the message presupposes the two poles as originally distinct. The same is true of the concern for the independence of the philosophical analysis. John Clayton, too, thinks in these terms; he is concerned with the mediation between two distinct realities.

One might try to defend Tillich without disabusing this presupposition. Such a procedure probably would be necessary if one were interested in defending the apologetic correlation, and this defense might even be successful. I wish to move in a different direction, however. I wish to examine how the hermeneutical method of correlation fares when its elements—questions representing the structure of being and symbols representing the depth of the structure of being—are subjected to the condition of simultaneous independence and interdependence. My claim is that it succeeds admirably.

The hermeneutical correlation does not utilize philosophical analysis and religious symbols as representatives of the cultural situation on the one hand and the Christian message on the other. Rather, it understands the philosophical questions as articulations of the structure of being that is the

---

[113]Ibid., 236.

[114]See ibid., 236-49.

condition of the possibility for one's experiencing anything at all, and understands the Christian symbols as providing a perspective on the depth of that structure. The questions do articulate *particular* components of that structure, and the Christian symbols do disclose a *particular* perspective on being-itself, a perspective impossible without the appearance of these symbols at certain points in history. But that the hermeneutical correlation's elements do function in such a manner does not alter their fundamental makeup: they do not represent two distinct entities called cultural situation and Christian message but rather the structure of finite being and the Christian grasp of the depth of that structure. This fact will hardly alleviate the anxieties of someone like Hamilton, for this formal, structural account of the relationship between the poles of the correlation further emphasizes the mutual dependence of the poles. In other words, the success of the hermeneutical correlation with respect to the condition of independence and interdependence, as I see it, does not consist in its ability to allay the fears of a Hamilton. Rather, the hermeneutical correlation succeeds in maintaining both the independence and the interdependence of its elements *in a manner appropriate to the special task it is designed to accomplish.*

The hermeneutical correlation does involve a more fundamental mutual dependence of its elements than does the apologetic. In the apologetic correlation, the questions asked affect the form of the answers, and the answers given affect the form of the questions. But the mutual dependence entailed in the hermeneutical correlation has to do not only with the *method* itself but also with the nature of the reality the method is applied to. The structure of finite being is the structure that it is only as grounded in being-itself; it is dependent upon being-itself as its unconditional depth. Similarly, being-itself can be defined only in terms of the structure of finite being; it is the ground of that structure. By juxtaposing questions expressing the structure of finite being with answers expressing being-itself, the hermeneutical correlation reflects this mutual dependence.

But the view of reality presupposed in the hermeneutical correlation also adds a significant degree of independence to the equation. While the structure of finite being and being-itself are what they are only in relation to one another, nonetheless one cannot be reduced to the other, for being-itself is unconditionally "beyond" the self-world structure of being. Now it seems to me that the hermeneutical version of correlation is not only based upon a view of reality in which being-itself is distinguishable from the structure it grounds, but that in operation it succeeds in accurately representing and maintaining that distinction. Indeed, the purpose of the hermeneutical correlation, as a correlation, is to provide an *indirect* account of the awareness, mediated by certain religious symbols, of being-itself.

I think that it has been shown above that the hermeneutical method of correlation does provide such an indirect account. This means, of course, that it offers a way of interpreting religious symbols that does not reduce what they represent to something less than being-itself—being-itself is not reduced to the structure of finite being—while providing some information about the content of the symbols—it specifies the place within the finite structure of being from which a symbol gives a view of being-itself. Thus, although being-itself is a dimension of reality beyond conceptualization, one is no longer condemned to silence before it.

Furthermore, it should be apparent why the charge does not arise here that religion is holding philosophy captive. In the apologetic correlation, the supposition that the philosophical questions represent the contemporary culture suggests that those questions should be "philosophical" in the sense that they should represent schools of philosophy existing within that culture. The questions should, in other words, be taken from the work of those in the culture who deem themselves academic philosophers and who distinguish their work from theology. As a result, difficulties arise if the questions appear to spring at least in part from a theological interest.

But "philosophical" means something different in the context of the hermeneutical correlation. Philosophy in that context is distinguished from religion as a description of the structure of reality over against the concern with that dimension of reality beyond conceptualization. Here, philosophy is a kind of thinking that pertains to the structure of finite being rather than a specific academic discipline. Hence, the obvious theological concern in some of Tillich's philosophical questions does not negate the integrity of philosophy as it is understood in the context of the hermeneutical correlation.

The hermeneutical correlation thus succeeds in maintaining, in a manner appropriate to its task, both the independence and the interdependence of the two poles of the correlation. It answers the critics surveyed here not by disproving their judgments about the apologetic correlation, although a defender of Tillich might well be able to do that, but by uncovering a dimension of Tillich's method previously unconsidered, a dimension in which the balance between dependence and interdependence is clearly maintained.

The hermeneutical correlation not only answers those who worry that the independence of one or both of the two poles will be compromised, it also puts John Clayton's worry in a new light. Clayton has interpreted Tillich's explicit method of correlation in terms of the need to mediate between contemporary culture and the Christian message. Understandably, he therefore believes there must be a reciprocal relation between the poles such that each is open to influence by the other. The culture Christianity resides in ought to be able to affect it. However, if the two poles of the correlation are conceived of in terms of structure and ground rather than of cultural situation and Christian message, one realizes that there is an aspect of Tillich's method of correlation whose task is not a matter of apologetics nor of "mediation" in the sense that the term is used within an apologetic context. In other words, Tillich's method of correlation succeeds in a way not recognized by the critics; it accomplishes its task without the alterations that someone like Clayton supposes it requires.

It has been shown that the hermeneutical correlation succeeds in maintaining both the independence and interdependence of its two poles and that it can perform an interpretive function the apologetic correlation cannot. Indeed, that this interpretive task is unfinished after the apologetic correlation has been carried out can cause one, it was suggested above, to attempt to translate a religious symbol directly into literal language. This defect of the apologetic correlation indicates that the hermeneutical correlation is important not only in its own right, but as an augmentation of the apologetic correlation.

But can the reverse also be said? That is, can one say that the apologetic correlation augments the hermeneutical? At least in one respect it seems that one can. Because the hermeneutical correlation juxtaposes the Christian symbols with the structure of being rather than with a cultural situation, there is the danger that it may induce one to separate the import of the Christian faith from the concrete historical world. As James Luther Adams demonstrates in his introduction to Tillich's *Political Expectation*, Tillich sought to combine a concern for the individual and the structure of his or her being with a concern for the social and political realm. In fact, Adams argues, persuasively, I believe, that because Tillich was concerned with this larger historical dimension of reality, he was able to take an earlier, more effective, and more morally responsible stand against Nazism than was taken by three other influential theological and philosophical thinkers of that era, namely, Rudolf Bultmann, Karl Barth, and Martin Heidegger.[115] Tillich himself complains that, paradoxical as it seems, Heidegger's notion of "historicity" actually abstracts from real history.[116]

Thus, it may be that the hermeneutical correlation should always be augmented by the apologetic, for the apologetic correlation is a necessary reminder that the ahistorical interpretations of symbols produced by the hermeneutical correlation always have historical *implications.* The interpretations themselves refer to the relatively invariant structure of being[117] rather than to a particular cultural situation, but for good or for ill, those interpretations will always be received in and applied to the actual historical world.

At the same time, the structural, ahistorical emphasis of the hermeneutical correlation can serve as a reminder that, while religious symbols are always received in and applicable to concrete historical and political circumstances, the import of those symbols, the reality of God as being-itself, should not be identified with those circumstances to the point of idolatry. Tillich learned a lesson along these lines when Emanuel Hirsch employed the notion of the *Kairos,* a notion that had been central to Tillich's own thinking, in such a way as to lend theological approval to the Nazi movement.[118]

A Summary of the Role of Empowerment

In the first three chapters, I traced the phenomenon of empowerment from Tillich's ontology, through his symbol theory, and into his method of correlation. I have shown, first, that, given the presuppositions of Tillich's phenomenological ontology, the experience of empowerment is to

------

[115]See James Luther Adams, "Introduction," in *Political Expectation,* vi-xx.

[116]See Paul Tillich, "The Political Meaning of Utopia," in *Political Expectation,* 146.

[117]See *ST,* 1:166-68.

[118]See John Clayton's discussion of this matter in *The Concept of Correlation,* 209-18.

be understood as giving to consciousness the presence of being-itself. Empowerment is thus the answer to a serious question about the notion of being-itself: if Tillich's being-itself cannot be described in positive, non-relational concepts, why suppose that the notion of being-itself is legitimate and that there is any reality corresponding to it? The phenomenon of empowerment provides a dialectical awareness of being-itself.

What does Tillich mean when he speaks of something serving as a symbol of being-itself? Sometimes, he is speaking in terms of symbolic propositions, that is, nonliteral assertions about being-itself. Given the nature of being-itself, the facts communicated in such assertions could only be negative or relational. But Tillich also speaks of a type of symbol that has nothing to do with propositions and facts but that instead serves as the concrete content of an ultimate concern. Such symbols represent or stand in for being-itself, directing consciousness beyond the limitation of being by nonbeing that characterizes the structure of finite being. This function in turn makes possible the phenomenon of empowerment, wherein a dialectical awareness of being-itself is given to consciousness. One knows that Christian symbols such as God, the Christ, and the Spiritual Presence mediate an awareness of being-itself, for they have this empowering quality.

If empowerment plays an important role in Tillich's ontology and in his treatment of religious symbols, it can be judged important to his method of correlation as well. Religious symbols can be understood as answering existential questions in that they empower what the questions seek. For example, the question "What is the source of courage?" is answered by the symbol of God, insofar as that symbol actually enables the courage to affirm one's being in spite of the threat of nonbeing. If the philosophical or existential questions used in the method of correlation are taken to represent a particular cultural situation, then the correlation is apologetic in nature, suggesting the relevance of Christian symbols to the plight of persons in that culture. If, on the other hand, the questions are taken as expressions of particular regions of the structure of finite being, then the method of correlation provides an indirect account of the particular awareness of being-itself afforded by a specific symbol. The fact of empowerment is the crucial objective datum required for describing this awareness.

According to this interpretation of the *Systematic Theology*, then, the phenomenon of empowerment plays a central role in the Tillichian system. Indeed, it could be termed its linchpin.

4

Symbol, Empowerment, and the World Religions

The investigation thus far suggests that the phenomenon of empowerment can be interpreted as a unifying thread running throughout Tillich's system, linking such elements of the system as Tillich's ontology and his symbol theory. This alliance between Tillich's ontology and his theory of symbols accounts for some of the most fascinating possibilities offered by his thought. It has shown itself to be useful in constructing a post-theistic religious philosophy, for it allows Tillich to say that the notion of God embraced by Christian theism, along with its ancillary concepts, is in fact a symbol for a reality ontologically more fundamental than the Supreme Being to which the notion of God refers literally.

A second, equally fascinating aspect of this alliance concerns the attempt to create a so-called world theology. Tillich's position is promising as the basis for a world theology in that it enables one to claim that differences among world religions are a function of the religions' using different symbols to point to the same ultimate reality; the differing content of two religions impedes a unifying perspective only if one fails to recognize that the content in each operates symbolically and points to something beyond that which it signifies literally. Tillich himself never detailed how the system set forth in the *Systematic Theology* could be used in this regard, though in his Bampton Lectures (given at Columbia University in 1961 and published as *Christianity and the Encounter of the World Religions*), he did explore the possibility of dialogue among world religions, and in his last public address, "The Significance of the History of Religions for the Systematic Theologian" (delivered at the University of Chicago in 1965 less than two weeks before his death), he suggested some preliminary steps in constructing a world theology.

In this chapter, I wish to point out the peculiar strengths of the method developed by Tillich in his *Systematic Theology* for articulating a world theology. If these strengths do derive from the alliance between Tillich's ontology and his symbol theory, and if that alliance can be approached via the phenomenon of empowerment, then it will be appropriate to concentrate here upon those aspects of Tillich's system connected with empowerment, that is, those aspects treated in the first three chapters. I shall summarize the preliminary steps Tillich himself sets forth in "The Significance of the History of Religions for the Systematic Theologian," augmenting that summary with references to his other works. Then, in order to orient the discussion, I shall discuss some proposals for a world theology that have been advanced in the last decade. This summary and orientation will prepare the way for showing how those aspects of Tillich's system explored in the first three chapters might be utilized to construct a world theology.

Preliminary Steps
Suggested by Tillich

The sort of world theology Tillich is interested in is not one that would claim to stand in a position of omniscient objectivity above all traditional religions. Rather, Tillich suggests that one must create a theology from the perspective of a particular tradition. Thus, he asserts that a theology should remain rooted in its "experiential basis."

> Without this, no theology at all is possible. But it tries to formulate the basic experiences which are universally valid in universally valid statements. The universality of a religious statement does not lie in an all-embracing abstraction which would destroy religion as such, but it lies in the depths of every concrete religion. Above all it lies in the openness

to spiritual freedom both from one's own foundation and for one's own foundation.[1]

Again,

> Christianity will be a bearer of the religious answer as long as it breaks through its own particularity. The way to achieve this is not to relinquish one's religious tradition for the sake of a universal concept which would be nothing but a concept. The way is to penetrate into the depth of one's own religion, in devotion, thought and action. In the depth of every living religion there is a point at which the religion itself loses its importance, and that to which it points breaks through its particularity, elevating it to spiritual freedom and with it to a vision of the spiritual presence in other expressions of the ultimate meaning of man's existence. This is what Christianity must see in the present encounter of the world religions.[2]

The relative weight Tillich assigns to this contention—that a world theological concern does not reject the particular and concrete but sees the universal through the particular—is demonstrated by the above quotations' positions as conclusions to Tillich's two most important essays on the world religions. However, while a Christian thinker, for example, may operate from a recognizably Christian perspective, that thinker need not assume that Christianity is superior to other faiths; it ought to be possible to see from the Christian perspective that the Christian tradition must take its place not above but beside other religious traditions within a universal history of religions.

What, then, of the specific steps proposed by Tillich in "The Significance of the History of Religions for the Systematic Theologian"?[3] He be-

------

[1]Paul Tillich, "The Significance of the History of Religions for the Systematic Theologian," in *The Future of Religions*, ed. Jerald C. Brauer (Westport CT: Greenwood Press, 1976) 94.

[2]Paul Tillich, *Christianity and the Encounter of the World Religions* (New York: Columbia University Press, 1963) 97. Compare pp. 2-3, 27-29.

[3]"The Significance of the History of Religions" is aimed not only at the question of how Christian theology ought to respond to the world's religions but also at the challenge posed by the so-called secular or death of God theology that received much attention in the 1960s. This summary will concentrate upon the former issue, since the latter falls outside of the concerns of this chapter.

gins by asserting that theologians who take seriously the topic suggested by the title of the address must abjure theology that rejects unconditionally all religions other than their own. The type of theology Tillich criticizes is expressed, in the twentieth-century, in a position attributed to Karl Barth by some of his followers: *faith* in response to the revelation of God in Jesus Christ must be distinguished from *religion.* While faith in God's self-revelation in Christ is a response to the divine initiative, religion is a futile attempt on the part of human beings to reach God through their own efforts. Even Christianity can be taken as a religion and must be contrasted with Christian faith. All non-Christian religious traditions are of course examples of religion, not of Christian faith.

Against this perspective, Tillich urges the acceptance of five "systematic presuppositions":[4] first, revelation is present in all religions. Consonant with the claim that the phenomenon of empowerment is central to Tillich's thought, Tillich refers here to a revelation as "a particular kind of experience which always implies saving powers."[5]

Second, because of human finitude and estrangement, revelation is always received in a distorted form. Apparently, then, no one religion can claim to have a perfect grasp of the reality revealed.

Third, not only are there particular revelatory experiences throughout human history, but there is also "a revelatory process in which the limits of adaptation and the failures of distortion are subjected to criticism."[6] The criticism takes three forms, namely, the mystical, the prophetic, and the secular.

Fourth, there *may* be—Tillich does not wish to suggest certainty on this point—"a central event in the history of religions which unites the positive results of those critical developments in the history of religion in and under which revelatory experiences are going on."[7] Such an event would make possible a concrete theology with universal significance.

Fifth, the sacred is not an element alongside the secular but, rather, is the depth of the secular. The sacred stands in judgment over the secular,

---

[4]Tillich, "History of Religions," 81.

[5]Ibid.

[6]Ibid.

[7]Ibid.

but the secular must, at the same time, be taken up into the sacred as a moment of self-criticism.

The necessity of these five systematic presuppositions noted, Tillich moves on to sketch the content of a world theology, or a "theology of the history of religion."[8] He suggests a "dynamic-typological" approach[9] that divides religion into three main elements. The first element is the sacramental basis of all religions, that is, the experience of the Holy within finite reality. The second element is critical, the mystical tendency. In a separate essay, Tillich says that mystical religiousness emphasizes the participation pole of the ontological structure; it is expressed in "symbols of proceeding from and receding into the One."[10] Mysticism has a critical function in that it creates an attitude in which one is unsatisfied with the concrete expressions of the Holy or ultimate. Thus, the mystical element fights the demonic temptation to identify a particular embodiment of ultimate reality with that reality itself. The third element is the ethical or prophetic element, the element of "ought to be" that, for example, criticizes the sacramental when it denies justice in the name of holiness. Here again a demonic tendency is countered, justifying the characterization of the prophetic element as critical in function. Elsewhere Tillich explains that prophetic religiousness emphasizes the individualization pole of the ontological structure; it is expressed in "symbols of being created by and reunited with the Ground of Being."[11]

According to the "dynamic-typological" approach, all religions possess the three elements listed,[12] but one element usually predominates in

---

[8]Ibid., 84.

[9]Ibid., 86.

[10]Paul Tillich, "Symbols of Eternal Life," *Harvard Divinity Bulletin* 26 (April 1962): 4.

[11]Ibid.

[12]One might read secularization as a fourth element alongside the mystical and the prophetic as one more critical principle (see Tillich, "History of Religions," 81, 89). There is, as Huston Smith points out, an ambiguity here, perhaps attributable to the editor's reconstruction of Tillich's address: "On pages 86-89 the three elements in religious experience get tangled, if not scrambled, with the three checks against religious demonization." Huston Smith, "Review of Paul Tillich, *The Future of Religions*," *Journal of Religion* 47 (April 1967): 185.

each individual religion, thereby creating a particular religious *type*. So, for example, Christianity, although possessing all three elements, can be said to be a prophetic type of religion, while Buddhism, though consti- tuted too by all three elements, represents the mystical type.[13]

Tillich's approach also holds that the positive and negative relation of the three elements in the history of religions gives that history a *dy- namic* quality. Tillich suggests that, on the basis of this dynamic-typolog- ical approach to religion, it is possible to specify a *telos* of the history of religions. That *telos* is the union of the sacramental, mystical, and pro- phetic elements into "the Religion of the Concrete Spirit."[14] In such a re- ligion, the three elements perfectly balance one another so that the sacramental element does not lead to demonic distortion—the elevation of the finite to ultimate significance—while at the same time, the mystical element does not destroy the necessary concreteness of religion and the prophetic element does not turn religion into mere secular moralism. By speaking of this Religion of the Concrete Spirit as the *telos* of the history of religions, Tillich does not wish to suggest that it is a matter of future expectation, that history is moving toward its realization within time. In- stead, he sees it as an eternal goal that is realized in a fragmentary way in many places in the history of religions. This notion of the fragmentary manifestation of the Religion of the Concrete Spirit throughout history adds specificity to the third systematic presupposition noted above (that there is a revelatory process in history in which distortions of religion are criticized).

From the Christian perspective, the death of the Christ on the cross, as the divine victory over demonic forces, serves as the norm for validating apparent manifestations of the Religion of the Concrete Spirit:

> The criterion for us as Christians is the event of the cross. That which
> has happened there in a symbolic way, which gives the criterion, also
> happens fragmentarily in other places, in other moments, has hap-

---

[13]See Tillich, *Christianity and the Encounter of the World Religions*, 58-75.

[14]Tillich, "History of Religions," 87.

pened and will happen even though they are not historically or empirically connected with the cross.[15]

This statement is consistent with Tillich's claim, discussed in chapter 2, that the symbol of the cross possesses an internal check against demonic distortion; it seems to suggest that the Christ-event could be the central event in the history of religions that Tillich called a possibility in his fourth systematic presupposition.[16]

In the last section of his address, Tillich considers "the interpretation of the theological tradition in the light of religious phenomena."[17] His intention is to show how the theology of a particular tradition can come to understand itself as a part of the universal history of religions, not only in the abstract terms provided by the dynamic-typological approach and the concept of the Religion of the Concrete Spirit, but in terms of the concrete data of the history of human religious experience and practice. Toward this end, theology must take a methodological clue from those who study the history of religions and avoid the blindness toward concrete, historical reality characteristic of both supernatural and natural theology. The supernatural theology of Protestant orthodoxy viewed the content of theology as deriving directly from divine revelation; there was no preparation in history for theological doctrines. Similarly, natural theology usually tries to derive theological propositions from the invariant structure of reality

---

[15]Ibid., 89. Compare Tillich, *Christianity and the Encounter of the World Religions*, 79-82.

[16]The suggestion that the Christ-event (and the resultant symbol of the cross) might be the central event in the history of religions may seem to contradict the claim that Tillich's work on the world religions involves a decidedly Christian perspective in which Christianity is nonetheless seen not to be superior. But note, first, that in the quotation just cited Tillich concedes that what happened in the event of the cross can happen elsewhere. Second, the point of the symbol of the cross is that no finite manifestation of being-itself is itself ultimate; the "superiority" of the symbol of the cross is its self-negating character. This second observation applies even to those earlier discussions of the symbol of the cross wherein Tillich seems to suggest that Christianity is unique in possessing such a symbol. See *Dynamics of Faith*, 97-98.

[17]Tillich, "History of Religions," 91.

and mind; there is no reference to the development of religious ideas and practices in history.

In contrast to the methods of supernatural and natural theology, what Tillich calls the method of the history of religions proceeds in five steps:[18] first, it uses the material of a particular religious tradition as existentially experienced by theologians in that tradition. Second, borrowing from natural theology's method, it analyzes mind and reality in order to situate the religious question within human experience. Third, it presents a phenomenology of religion that allows the symbols, rites, ideas, and activities making up the history of religions to show themselves. Fourth, the method points out how these symbols, rites, ideas, and activities relate to traditional theological concepts. Finally, the reinterpreted concepts are placed within the framework of religious and secular history and, most importantly, within the framework of the present religious and cultural situation. When these five steps have been carried out, one can see how the symbols, concepts, and rites of one's tradition emerge out of a rich, concrete historical milieu and how they relate to the present cultural situation.

How might the method Tillich developed in his *Systematic Theology* augment his suggestions for constructing a theology of the history of religions? In order to answer this question, one must consider first some recent attempts at a world theology.

Recent Attempts
at a World Theology

It is an unfortunate fact that while many Christian thinkers have in recent years addressed the issue of the relationship between Christianity

---

[18]It is unclear whether Tillich is proposing here a new method that combines the disciplines traditionally called the history of religions and systematic theology, or whether he simply intends to describe the history of religions and to suggest how theology could benefit from a knowledge of it. Howard Burkle argues that Tillich sees himself as describing the history of religions but that what he describes ought to be understood as the total task of religious studies. See "Tillich's 'Dynamic-Typological' Approach to the History of Religions," *Journal of the American Academy of Religion* 49 (June 1981): 182.

and other faiths and have expressed a good deal of appreciation for those non-Christian religions, few have been able to free themselves from a belief in Christian superiority to the degree necessary for legitimately undertaking a *world* theology.[19] Even such prominent figures on the contemporary theological scene as Karl Rahner, Hans Küng, Jürgen Moltmann, and Wolfhart Pannenberg must be indicted, a conclusion reenforced by surveys made by Paul Knitter and John Cobb.[20] Indeed, in Cobb's survey he concludes, "Of all the major figures treated here only Tillich seems to be completely exempt."[21] This is not to say, of course, that there have been no recent worthy attempts at a world theology other than Tillich's; while the proposals for a genuine world theology have been relatively few, those few have often been deserving of study. I wish to study some of those proposals here, for such a consideration, I think, will help to clarify the nature of Tillich's contribution. I shall treat three basic "types" of world theology and the proponents of those types.

There are two reasons for beginning with what I shall call the "metaphysical" type of world theology, that which claims to disclose a fundamental unity among the world religions by pointing to some ultimate dimension of reality that is beyond literal description and that all world religions give witness to from their varying, finite perspectives. First, the

---

[19]As examples, see Diogenes Allen, "A Christian Theology of Other Faiths," *Theology Today* 38 (October 1981): 305-13; Charles Davis, *Christ and the World Religions* (London: Hodder and Stroughton, 1970); R. C. Zaehner, "Religious Truth," in *Truth and Dialogue: The Relationship between World Religions,* ed. John Hick (London: Sheldon Press, 1974) 1-19.

[20]See Paul Knitter, "What is German Protestant Theology Saying About the Non-Christian Religions?" *Neue Zeitschrift für systematische Theologie und Religionsphilosphie* 15 (1973): 38-64, and "European Protestant and Catholic Approaches to the World Religions: Complements and Contrasts," *Journal of Ecumenical Studies* 12 (Winter 1975): 13-28; John B. Cobb, *Beyond Dialogue: Toward a Mutual Transformation of Christianity and Buddhism* (Philadelphia: Fortress Press, 1982) 15-47.

[21]Cobb, *Beyond Dialogue*, 41. Contrast this judgment of Tillich with Knitter's misjudgment, a misjudgment attributable to Knitter's giving insufficient weight to Tillich's later works on the world religions. See "European Protestant and Catholic Approaches to the World Religions," 22-23. Compare note 16 above.

sort of world theology that can be built upon Tillichian presuppositions appears to be an example of this type, though I shall argue that a Tillichian world theology can significantly modify the standard metaphysical approach. Second, there is a sense in which the other two types to be discussed presuppose the metaphysical approach; the metaphysical approach always seems to be required to complete a world theology. Thus, the metaphysical approach will serve as a kind of center of gravity in the discussion that follows.

The metaphysical approach to a world theology is not, of course, a creation of the last decade, as anyone familiar with Hindu thought, for example, can attest. It has, however, received a good deal of attention in the West in recent years. A case in point is the discussion generated by the reprinting in 1975 of Frithjof Schuon's *Transcendent Unity of Religions*.[22] Schuon's argument can be seen as a paradigm of the metaphysical approach. According to Schuon, while the world's religions differ from one another on the "exoteric" level, they converge on the higher or "esoteric" level. That is, one who has attained the esoteric level recognizes that the divine is ineffable, lying beyond the realm available to ordinary thinking and thus beyond the realm of reality about which distinctions can be made. The esoteric position is reached through a mystical state of consciousness in which the subject-object duality is transcended, and, having arrived at that position, one can see that the debate—for instance, between Christian and Buddhist—about the character of ultimate reality operates at a merely preliminary level.

Another proponent of the metaphysical approach is the British philosopher of religion John Hick.[23] Hick, utilizing a Kantian distinction in

---

[22]See, for example, Richard C. Bush, "Frithjof Schuon's *The Transcendent Unity of Religions*: Con," and Huston Smith's "Pro" in *Journal of the American Academy of Religion* 44 (December 1976): 715-24. Smith wrote the introduction to the new edition of Schuon's book, and Schuon's influence is evident in Smith's own *Forgotten Truth: The Primordial Tradition* (New York: Harper and Row, 1976).

[23]See John Hick, "Towards a Philosophy of Religious Pluralism," *Neue Zeitschrift für systematische Theologie und Religionsphilosophie* 22 (1980): 131-49, and *God Has Many Names: Britain's New Religious Pluralism* (London: Macmillan, 1980).

a non-Kantian fashion, suggests that one ought to distinguish between the transcendent as noumenon and its phenomenal manifestations. No one can experience "God" *an sich* but only as filtered through his or her own mental equipment and peculiar situation. All religions may, according to Hick, intend the same noumenal God, but the religions differ from one another due to differing phenomenal adumbrations of him. Thus, for example, the experience of God as personal and the experience of him as nonpersonal are equally valid, both being merely phenomenal. Here Hick differs from Schuon, for whereas Schuon thinks according to a hierarchical scheme in which the intuition of God as nonpersonal is superior to and more accurate than the experience of God as personal, Hick maintains that the differing perspectives need not be related to one another as higher and lower; no one attains knowledge of the divine noumenon.[24]

There is, unfortunately, one outstanding weakness in this metaphysical approach to a world theology. One might at first suppose that that weakness concerns the danger of disregarding the concrete elements of religion. But someone like Schuon can, presumably, avoid this danger by emphasizing the necessity of concrete rites, symbols, and doctrines as stepping stones to the esoteric plane, and Hick can point to the necessity of the concrete in the phenomenal contact with the divine, the only contact available. The real drawback to this approach, I believe, is the nonverifiability of the claim that all religions, or at least many, intend a single metaphysical reality.

The question here is not whether such a reality exists but rather what the relation of the world's religions is to such a reality if it does exist. Even if one granted that the notion of an ineffable ultimate beyond the subject-object divide, or a divine noumenon ever shielded from one by one's modes of experiencing, would not violate the integrity of any of the world's religious traditions if introduced there, how would one judge the claim that such an ultimate is, whether or not it exists, in fact the reality implicitly intended by each of the world's major religions? Surely it does not follow that if all religions *ought* to have this ultimate as the object of their quest then they *do*. After all, most adherents of the world's religions are un-

---

[24]There is a sense in which Hick undercuts himself here, for he must also admit that God cannot be personal *an sich*. Is not the nonpersonal view thus more accurate after all? See "Towards a Philosophy of Religious Pluralism," 143-46.

aware of this ultimate; their concept of what is ultimate is usually quite different.

Someone like Schuon or Hick apparently must operate by fiat, simply declaring that the ineffable ultimate he or she envisions is the center of all human religiousness.[25] Indeed, Hick himself at one point seems to admit to a closely related problem:

> I have just referred to the different world religions, with their different images of God. Our question concerns the relative adequacy or value of these images, both theistic and nontheistic. For it is clearly possible that they are not all equally adequate, but that some mediate God to mankind better than others. . . . But by what criteria do we assess such images; and how do we establish such criteria?[26]

Hick leaves his question unanswered. To connect his question and the objection raised here, if one cannot judge the relative adequacy of supposed responses to the reality of the noumenal God, how can one judge whether they *are* responses called forth by that noumenal God?

The problem of nonverifiability associated with the metaphysical approach to world theology makes what can be called the "personalist" approach seem, at least initially, quite attractive. If one cannot demonstrate that a fundamental unity exists among the world's religions by virtue of a common metaphysical goal, why not turn from the metaphysical to the personal, that is, to the characteristics of the individual's religious quest? Might not an important unity be found on this more mundane stratum of reality?

The personalist approach has been argued forcefully by Wilfred Cantwell Smith. Smith finds the most important common element of human religiousness—he dislikes the term *religion*, viewing it as a fallacious reification—in the way people of different religious traditions live out their lives; they share a common way of being in the world, a way Smith calls "faith." This faith, different in form but not in kind as it appears in the lives of religious individuals, is a way of life that saves one "from nihilism,

------

[25]Compare William A. Christian, *Oppositions of Religious Doctrines: A Study in the Logic of Dialogue among Religions* (New York: Herder and Herder, 1972) 110-22.

[26]Hick, "Towards a Philosophy of Religious Pluralism," 149.

from alienation, anomie, despair; from the bleak despondency of mean-
inglessness."[27] For Smith, it is absurd to speak of religious traditions being
true or false in and of themselves. Rather, a tradition can become true in
the life of an individual if it makes this kind of saving faith possible for
him or her, and it can become false for an individual if it proves destructive to that person.[28]

Smith's position is useful—especially when one recalls the primary
weakness of the metaphysical approach—in that it offers some empirical
evidence, on the level of what he calls "faith," for the unity of the world's
religious traditions. One can observe that some persons do escape destructive forces such as nihilism, alienation, anomie, despair, and meaning-
lessness. And while it would probably be impossible to prove in any
particular case that a person's religious faith made that escape possible, that
conclusion can at least be rendered quite likely, if by no other means than
the testimony of the individual involved. So one may conclude that Smith
can provide evidence for the claim that the world's religious traditions have
in common the potential for providing a way of life that allows persons to
overcome forces such as despair.

Smith goes on to say that living life religiously involves living in relation to a transcendent reality.[29] Here a problem arises. On the one hand,
it does seem that Smith must add to his description of faith this notion of
a transcendent reference; otherwise his theology will be reductionistic—it
will interpret the heart of the religious life as being less ontologically significant than most religious persons suppose it to be. But, on the other
hand, unity among the world's religions on the level of a transcendent reference cannot be established empirically. Perhaps empirical evidence can
show that all of the major religious traditions of the world assume *some*
transmundane reality. But that snippet of agreement is general, even vac-
uous. Is there any substantial, significant common element to be discov-
ered in the notions of God the Father, Nirvana, Brahman, and the Tao,

---

[27]Wilfred Cantwell Smith, *Towards a World Theology: Faith and the Comparative History of Religion* (Philadelphia: Westminster, 1981) 168.

[28]See ibid., 93-94, and Wilfred Cantwell Smith, "Can Religions Be True or
False?" in *Questions of Religious Truth* (New York: Scribners, 1967) 65-96.

[29]See Smith, *Towards a World Theology,* 26-27, 35, 127, 186.

for example? Thus, Smith's personalist position forces one to look back toward the metaphysical type in which the notions of God the Father, Nirvana, Brahman, and the Tao can be seen as different ciphers for a single reality ontologically more fundamental than what any describes if taken literally.

The idea that the personalist approach to world theology ultimately requires the metaphysical approach for its completion is reinforced by an essay of Raimundo Panikkar. In "Faith and Belief," Panikkar too concentrates on the personal dimension of religion as the first place one should seek for unity among the world religions, and he distinguishes between the personal act of *faith* and the objectification of that act in *belief*. Belief is "an intellectual, emotional and cultural embodiment" of faith.[30] Thus, two persons with very different beliefs—suppose one person is a theist and the other an atheist—could in fact share the same faith.

> Both believe in truth, but the phrase 'God exists' sums up the truth for one Man, while for the other the phrase 'God does not exist' sums it up. At this point the more exact statement enters: Both have *faith* in the truth, but for the one this faith expresses itself in the *belief* that 'God exists', while for the other it expresses itself in the contrary proposition, 'God does not exist'.[31]

But Panikkar has no desire to reduce religion to subjectivity. The truth that faith intends is a reality beyond the merely human realm.

> The main function of faith is to connect me with transcendence, with what stands above, with what I am not (yet). Faith is the connection with the beyond, however you choose to envision it. So one thing faith effects is salvation: The business of faith is preeminently to save Man.[32]

A problem arises here. Theoretically, persons could have the same faith while holding different beliefs, if faith is understood as a matter simply of personal disposition. But when the fact that faith entails a transcendent reference is added to the subjective characteristics of faith,

---

[30]Raimundo Panikkar, "Faith and Belief," in *The Intrareligious Dialogue* (New York: Paulist Press, 1978) 12.

[31]Ibid., 8.

[32]Ibid., 18.

complications arise, for now an objective reality enters the picture. Wouldn't faith then be said to possess a cognitive component, a component that would be expressed in one's *belief*? Wouldn't it then follow that if one's belief were significantly different from the belief of one's neighbor such a disparity would reflect an important difference in the respective acts of faith? How can such difficulties be overcome?

They can be overcome if one assumes that because the transcendent intended by all true faith is beyond human comprehension and unavailable to literal description, the transcendent reality intended by faith could be legitimately thought and expressed in many different forms. In other words, the metaphysical approach to world theology appears again on the scene, though Panikkar grafts it onto the personalist approach by emphasizing the ineffability of the transcendent via a discussion of the inexhaustibility of *faith*: "Faith may lend itself more or less to ideation, but no set of words, no expression, can ever exhaust it."[33] Faith is "ever transcendent, unutterable and open."[34]

A third type of world theology is, in a sense, more conservative than the metaphysical and the personalist types. The proponents of this third type usually do not look for some single stratum within the world's religions that would suggest an essential unity among them. Instead, they prefer to consider the world's religious traditions in more detail and to explore those points at which insights of one tradition might be usefully juxtaposed with those of another in such a way that the traditions can learn from one another. Scholars who embark upon this third approach envision the relationship between the religions they study as one of *complementarity*, a term that surfaces frequently in their writing.

Perhaps the most impressive recent work embracing the way of complementarity is John Cobb's *Beyond Dialogue: Toward a Mutual Transformation of Christianity and Buddhism*.[35] Utilizing his own by now familiar version of a Whiteheadian process metaphysic as a foundation, Cobb explores what Christianity can learn from Buddhism on such topics

----

[33]Ibid.

[34]Ibid., 12.

[35]For Cobb's use of the term *complementarity* see *Beyond Dialogue*, 67.

as attachment or craving, the self, ultimate reality, and time. Similarly, he considers several insights Buddhism might gain from Christianity.

The claim that Buddhism and Christianity are complementary is also advanced, though in a less disciplined, more offhand manner, by Ninian Smart in his *Beyond Ideology: Religion and the Future of Western Civilization.*[36] The notion of complementarity also arises in John A. T. Robinson's discussion of certain pairs of religious perspectives—for example, the ultimate as personal versus the ultimate as nonpersonal—which Robinson believes exist within individual religious traditions although they are usually thought of as tensions that arise between two different traditions.[37] Finally, there is Robley Whitson, who speaks of complementarity in discussing an impending convergence among the world religions that he believes will involve both unity and pluralism.[38]

What problems are inherent to complementarity? If, on the one hand, complementarity is taken in a relatively weak sense, meaning only an attempt to balance extremes in one tradition through input from others, then it cannot serve as the basis for a world theology. One could, for example, remain essentially a Christian triumphalist while allowing that Buddhism might have something to teach the Christian about the nature of attachment and craving.

If, on the other hand, complementarity is taken in a strong sense, it may presuppose the metaphysical approach. Are the Christian version of the ultimate as a personal Supreme Being and the Buddhist notion of Nirvana complementary in the same way that, for example, a wave model of light and a particle model are complementary? If so, might one not conclude that the Christian notion of God and the Buddhist notion of Nirvana are both symbolic expressions of some dimension of reality lying beyond literal description? The metaphysical approach seems necessary to a "strong" interpretation of complementarity.

------

[36]See Ninian Smart, *Beyond Ideology: Religion and the Future of Western Civilization* (New York: Harper and Row, 1981) 106-36, 198-207, 309-13.

[37]Robinson invokes the notion of complementarity on pp. 14-15 of *Truth is Two-Eyed* (Philadelphia: Westminster, 1979).

[38]See Robley Edward Whitson, *The Coming Convergence of World Religions* (New York: Newman Press, 1971) 124-26.

Organizing recent discussions on world theology into these three basic approaches risks shortchanging the perspectives of individual thinkers by forcing them into the mold of an ideal type. The risk, however, seems worthwhile, for the procedure is useful in mapping out Tillich's place in contemporary discussion. His potential contributions to this discussion can now be evaluated.

Tillich's Hermeneutical Method as an Avenue to a World Theology

How might the method worked out in the *Systematic Theology* be added to the framework suggested in "The Significance of the History of Religions" to create a full-blown Tillichian world theology? Tillich defines the essence of religion as ultimate concern.[39] Genuine ultimate concern and hence genuine religion involve not only a subjective pole—the act of concern—but an objective pole—being-itself—as well. Because being-itself can be made present to consciousness only through the medium of symbols, it is evident how the Religion of the Concrete Spirit can be defined as the *telos* of all genuine religion.

The first element in that *telos* is the sacramental, for being-itself always requires symbolic mediation. The unconditional must be capable of representation by the finite. But this necessity creates a danger: one may come to believe that the finite mediator of the ultimate is itself ultimate. This would be to forget the symbolic character of a symbol and to use it demonically. The Religion of the Concrete Spirit therefore balances the sacramental element with critical elements: the mystical and prophetic. Clearly, if religion is concern about being-itself, then the *telos* of religion ought to be something like the Religion of the Concrete Spirit.

As is evident from *Christianity and the Encounter of the World Religions* and "The Significance of the History of Religions," those entities traditionally termed the world religions are not excluded by Tillich from the realm of genuine religion. They are examples of authentic ultimate concern and thus their *telos* is the Religion of the Concrete Spirit. How is

----

[39]Tillich continues to use this definition when he speaks specifically of the world religions. See *Christianity and the Encounter of the World Religions*, 4.

a common *telos* possible for traditions with world views as seemingly divergent as those of Christianity and Theravada Buddhism?

Being-itself, the object of all valid religious consciousness, is the unconditional depth of the structure of being. The central concepts of traditions like Christianity and Buddhism can be understood as pointing beyond their own literal, conceptual meaning toward this depth. The Christian concept of the Supreme Being and the Buddhist concept of Nirvana, while conflicting as conceptual descriptions of ultimate reality, both can be taken as symbolic—that is, as the concrete content of ultimate concern mediating being-itself to consciousness. The differences between the two notions are differences in symbolic material. Differences in the kind of symbols used may suggest differing approaches to and perspectives on being-itself, but the same ultimate reality is intuited in either case.

This analysis of Tillich's position would seem to suggest that his thinking is a straightforward example of the metaphysical approach to a theology of the history of religions. It must indeed be understood as a variation of that approach, for it does argue for a common essence in the world's religions by pointing to a reality said to be ontologically more ultimate than that reality about which the world's religions disagree. But Tillich can avoid the danger cited in the metaphysical approach as represented by someone like Schuon or Hick. Recall the first of the five systematic presuppositions with which Tillich begins "The Significance of the History of Religions." That first presupposition is stated thus:

> Religions are based on something that is given to man wherever he lives. He is given a revelation, a particular kind of experience which always implies saving powers. One never can separate revelation and salvation. There are revealing and saving powers in all religions.[40]

The strengths of the metaphysical and the personalist approaches coalesce here. The saving powers manifested through a religious tradition are, as noted in the above discussion of Smith, open to something approaching empirical investigation. Revelation, on the other hand, suggests an ultimate reality. But given the presuppositions of Tillich's phenomenological ontology, there is a direct connection between these two realities: the phenomenon of religious empowerment gives the presence of

---

[40]Tillich, "History of Religions," 81.

being-itself to consciousness. Thus, there is a way for Tillich to verify his specification of the common essence of the world's religions, even though what he has specified is not a mundane entity but a transcendent ultimate. Do the world's religions all manifest some kind of empirically observable saving effect, some sort of empowerment? Tillich assumes so, while Smith suggests that it is demonstrable that they do. It seems likely, then, that when Tillich's brand of phenomenological analysis is brought to bear on such instances of empowerment, they will turn out to parallel that empowerment effected by Christian symbols, the religious form of empowerment that by transcending fundamental poles of the structure of being makes being-itself present to consciousness. Thus, while Tillich can be said to define religion as ultimate concern and to draw his description of the *telos* of religion—that is, the Religion of the Concrete Spirit—from that definition, he need not simply declare that the world religions find their common essence in this definition: he can offer what amounts to verification, given the terms of his system.

Moving from this general description to a more concrete level, one can see how the hermeneutical correlation could be utilized here. Suppose one looks at a particular notion within a particular religious tradition, for example, the notion of Nirvana as held by a Buddhist. One might concentrate on the testimonies of self-acknowledged Buddhists or on specific Buddhist texts. The following scenario seems plausible: the word *Nirvana* is found to mean the highest possible state of awareness, an enlightened consciousness through which suffering is transcended. How does this concept actually function in Buddhist piety? The Buddhist is aware of the conflict in himself or herself between the desire to escape the constant cycle of suffering and his or her apparent imprisonment within that cycle. But the teachings of the Buddha and the Buddhist tradition, which culminate in the concept of Nirvana, empower the Buddhist to escape the world of suffering at least fragmentarily.

The notion of Nirvana serves, then, not only as a concept describing the end-state toward which the Buddhist aspires but has not yet attained, but also as a source of empowerment that prods the Buddhist toward that same goal. This ability of the concept of Nirvana to empower the fragmentary realization of a state of consciousness in which the cycle of suffering is broken seems to suggest, in Tillich's terms, that that concept empowers something like the conquest of the ambiguities of life.[41] If one concluded that it did indeed empower that conquest, one would also have to conclude that it served as a symbol mediating being-itself to consciousness. This discovery would verify concretely the claim that Buddhism (or at least that part of Buddhism represented by the persons or texts consulted) and Christianity both point to the same ultimate reality.

If Tillich's hermeneutical method allows verification of his claim concerning the essence of a religious tradition—that is, allows one to show that a religion has being-itself as its object of concern—it ought also to allow location, via the hermeneutical correlation, of a non-Christian religious symbol like Nirvana. Thus, if Nirvana empowers the conquest of the ambiguities of life, the awareness mediated by the symbol of Nirvana should equal the awareness mediated by a Christian symbol empowering the conquest of ambiguity, for instance, the symbol Spiritual Presence or the symbol Kingdom of God; Nirvana should provide an awareness of being-itself from the perspective of the structure of being qua structure of life. Recall, however, that Tillich describes Buddhism as a religion of the mystical type and Christianity as a religion of the prophetic type. Indeed, at one point he refers to the symbol Nirvana, labeling it a mystical symbol and contrasting it with the symbol Kingdom of God, which he labels prophetic.[42] Unless this statement be taken to refer only to the material constituting the symbol and not to the awareness it mediates, one must conclude that although both symbols might empower the conquest of ambiguity, the respective awarenesses they mediate cannot be exactly the same.

---

[41]Note that Tillich refers to both Nirvana and the Kingdom of God as "symbols of eternal life" (see Tillich, "Symbols of Eternal Life"). In his *Systematic Theology*, Tillich places the symbol of the Kingdom of God, along with other Christian symbols related to eternal life, within the context of the conquest of the ambiguities of life (see *ST*, 3:300-423). (Tillich's usage is imprecise here: he can refer to the Kingdom of God as a symbol of eternal life, as he does in the article just cited, but he can also refer to the concept of eternal life as itself a symbol standing alongside the symbols Spiritual Presence and Kingdom of God. See, for example, *ST*, 3:108, 356-57.) This placement seems to suggest that Nirvana, if it empowers, must empower the conquest of ambiguity.

[42]See Tillich, "Symbols of Eternal Life."

Beginning as early as his thesis on "Mystik und Schuldbewusstein in Schellings philosophisches Entwicklung" and continuing throughout his career, Tillich criticized mysticism for tending to dissipate the self.[43] While a mystical symbol that empowers unambiguous life could not threaten the essential character of the self—unambiguous life results from a ground-edness in being-itself that allows both the self side and the world side of the ontological polarities to be as they essentially ought to be—such a symbol must, on Tillich's terms, involve a different sort of self-consciousness than a symbol such as the Kingdom of God. Thus, another element can be added to the Tillichian method: not only should one be able to specify the perspective from which a symbol provides an awareness of being-itself but also how the self is conscious of itself in that awareness.[44]

Thus, Tillich's method as worked out in the *Systematic Theology* should, on the one hand, be able to verify Tillich's claim that concern about being-itself is the common essence of the world's religions. But, on the other hand, it ought also to be able to uncover the peculiar characteristics of individual symbols, first, by locating, via the hermeneutical correlation, the awareness of being-itself they mediate, and, second, by specifying the type of self-consciousness given with that awareness. If the suggestion— made in the last section of "The Significance of the History of Reli-gions"—is added, that one study the concrete historical and cultural cir-cumstances in which particular symbols become symbols and develop, then

---

[43]See James Horner, "Tillich's Rejection of Absolute Mysticism," *Journal of Religion* 58 (1978): 130-39. Horner lists other complaints Tillich has against mysticism as well, including the charge that it is ahistorical. This latter criticism suggests an important difference between the symbol Nirvana and the symbol Kingdom of God. See chapter 3, note 67 above, and Tillich, "Symbols of Eternal Life."

[44]Surely it is possible for different degrees of self-consciousness to accom-pany different instances of the phenomenon of empowerment. If one focuses upon the power *itself*, then self-consciousness will be at a minimum, since the power in question is being-itself: one cannot be aware of the self as something over against being-itself, for that would require that being-itself become an object. If, on the other hand, one focuses on the power *as enabling unambiguous life*, then it ought to be possible to have an awareness of being-itself that is coupled with an aware-ness of the self.

the Tillichian method can be said to provide an account of the common essence of the world's religions and a threefold consideration of the unique characteristics of individual symbols. Justice is done to both the universal and the concrete dimensions of religion.[45]

True, the understanding provided by the Tillichian method is based on the presuppositions of a particular religious tradition. While Tillich's method does not presuppose that Christianity is superior to all other religions or that it is the *telos* of the history of religions, it does draw heavily upon Christian doctrine and experience. A Jewish commentator notes, for example, that

> unlike his description of man's 'essential being,' which is an ontological and phenomenological analysis of rare brilliance and carried through with immense dialectical skill, Tillich's portrait of what he calls man's 'estranged existence,' though it is also purportedly the result of objective philosophical analysis, must strike the Jewish reader as very heavily weighted with Christian presuppositions. It is, in fact, largely a transcript of the Christian doctrine of man's fall and sinfulness, with a considerable borrowing from Freud's psychoanalytic theory of neurosis.[46]

Nor would Tillich wish to deny that his comments on the world religions have a decidedly Christian perspective.

There is a way, however, in which the hermeneutical correlation can be applied so as to extend beyond the bounds of the interpretive categories of Christianity. It has been shown that the hermeneutical correlation might be used to understand non-Christian religions and their symbols by pro-

---

[45]For a negative and a positive judgment respectively upon whether Tillich is able to keep sight of both the universal and the particular dimensions of the world's religions, see John W. Bowker, "Can Differences Make a Difference? A Comment on Tillich's Proposals for Dialogue between Religions," *Journal of Theological Studies* 24 (April 1973): 158-88 and Ishmar Harris, "The Dilemma of the Universal and the Particular Nature of Religion," *Journal of Religious Thought* 37 (Spring-Summer 1980): 42-49. Note, however, that both articles deal only with those essays in which Tillich speaks explicitly about the world religions; there is no consideration of how the hermeneutical method developed in the *Systematic Theology* might be applied in the context of the world religions.

[46]Bernard Martin, "Paul Tillich and Judaism," *Judaism* 15 (Spring 1966): 186.

viding an indirect conceptual account of the awareness those symbols mediate. There is, however, yet another way of utilizing the hermeneutical correlation, a way that would be intended not to furnish a conceptual explanation of what a symbol makes present to consciousness but that would serve as a means of orienting one's thinking so that one would be in a position for a particular symbol to work as a symbol for one. This use of correlation would, in other words, move not from symbol to description but from description to symbol.

Returning once more to Nirvana as a symbol, suppose that it does not operate symbolically for one: it does not serve as a source of empowerment nor mediate an awareness of being-itself. The hermeneutical correlation tells one what the symbol of Nirvana empowers and what it mediates to persons for whom it does operate symbolically. One is then able to understand the question the symbol answers—the context in which it operates as a symbol—and this understanding may prepare one to experience the symbolic power of the notion of Nirvana. In other words, the correlation might let the symbol come alive by bringing to one's awareness the dimension of one's being that the symbol addresses.

There is no guarantee that the hermeneutical correlation can bring a symbol to life in this manner. A symbol's operation as a symbol depends upon a multitude of factors, conscious and unconscious, including the experiences of one and one's social group. But if the potential exists for something to operate as a living symbol, the hermeneutical correlation may serve as a catalyst to actualize that potential. This use of the hermeneutical correlation, however, takes the discussion beyond the confines of a theoretical interpretation of religious symbols and into the realm of actual participation in a religious tradition and its symbols.

Conclusion

Paul Tillich's post-theistic system might usefully be developed in the direction of a world theology, as was shown in the preceding chapter. The position worked out there suggests one avenue for present-day appropriation and adaptation of Tillich's theology. How might this investigation as a whole aid in the present-day appropriation of Tillich's theology?

The contours of Tillich's post-theistic interpretation of religion are attractive to many and provide a framework for contemporary theological reflection, but because his descriptions of being-itself are sprinkled with terms and concepts drawn from post-Kantian German philosophy, it is difficult for some contemporary thinkers to adopt Tillich's interpretation. I have tried to show that the phenomenon of empowerment is the experiential basis of Tillich's discussion of being-itself. If empowerment is the experiential root of Tillich's notion of being-itself and the linchpin of his post-theistic system, then one should be able to enter Tillich's system without first accepting all of the tenets of German idealism.

Note, first, that the negation of the negation of being as it appears in Tillich's theology is not a Hegelian dialectic but the dialectic of religious empowerment. Being-itself is given to consciousness via the empowerment to overcome a conflict within oneself constituted by two fundamental poles of the structure of finite being as those poles are present to consciousness. Further evidence that Tillich rejects a Hegelian approach to being-itself can be found in his doctrine of religious symbols: symbols of God as being-itself are not merely penultimate expressions of truth, inferior to philosophical concepts. Symbols are superior to philosophical concepts. And recall that, far from specifically pointing to the Absolute Spirit of German idealism, the phenomenon of religious empowerment seems only to require as its source an awareness of a dimension of reality that in some sense lies beyond the structure of finitude wherein being is negated by nonbeing.[1]

But if this exploration of the role of the phenomenon of empowerment in Tillich's system can clarify expressions and concepts puzzling to those unsympathetic to German idealism and can point to where Tillich is independent of that school, it would be foolish to suppose that Tillich can be removed from the idealist camp altogether. One need only recall Tillich's connection of being-itself with *essence*, for example, or his reference to it as the *ground* of being and the *true itself*, to realize how difficult it would be to think being-itself, even in negative and relational terms, without referring to some of the tenets of idealist ontology.

How, then, can this investigation go beyond clarification and aid in the contemporary adoption and development of Tillich's thought, considering the apparent aversion to idealism found in many circles today? It might be possible, given the centrality of empowerment in Tillich's system, to adopt the fundamental post-theistic insights of Tillich's theology along with their basis in empowerment and then to develop them away from idealism more decisively than Tillich does in his remarks on being-itself.

In order to see the phenomenon of empowerment as an experience that opens up a post-theistic goal for the religious quest, one must of course hold onto some parts of the theoretical framework Tillich constructs. For instance, to speak of empowerment as a dialectic transcending two fundamental poles of the ontological structure is to accept something at least akin to Tillich's description of the self-world structure of consciousness. But consider interpreting in a way other than Tillich's that which is given to awareness in the experience of religious empowerment—namely, the dimension of reality lying beyond the structure of finitude wherein being is countered by nonbeing.

Imagine two possible "radicalizations" of Tillich's position. The first might be termed a radicalization toward transcendence, the second a rad-

---

[1]See the discussion of the sub-roles of a representative symbol in chapter 1.

icalization toward immanence. Tillich's account of the dimension of reality beyond finitude, that is, his discussion of what he terms "being-itself," makes clear that this dimension of reality can be described only negatively or relationally. One might, then, choose to employ the *via negativa* more rigorously than does Tillich and thereby eschew any suggestion that God, the reality intuited in empowerment, can be thought of as the ideal ground of being. In fact, one could abandon not only the ontology apparently at work when Tillich describes being-itself; one could leave the realm of ontology altogether. Thus, God would not be identified with what is ontologically ultimate but would be "beyond" Being, beyond the ontologically ultimate.

A person of different philosophical sensibilities might want to move in the opposite direction, might want to accept the post-theistic component of Tillich's system and its basis in empowerment but then carry out a radicalization of Tillich's insights in the direction of immanence. Suppose that one claims that Tillich's post-theistic interpretation of the Christian faith does not require acceptance of anything more than the self-world structure of consciousness (which, if one does not go the route of a phenomenological ontology, need not even be identified with the structure of finite being but only with the structure of human being), that the dimension of reality lying "beyond" that structure is simply that structure itself considered as a *totality*. What does it mean to speak of the "essential" from which one stands estranged in "existence"? The self-world structure that is the precondition of human experience is as it essentially ought to be when each of the polar elements is balanced by its complement; estrangement appears when the poles break away from one another, as, for instance, when freedom degenerates into mere arbitrariness, destiny into mechanical necessity. In order to account for the essence-existence divide, one does not need to refer to some variation upon the Platonic heaven but only to consider the self-world structure of consciousness, on the one hand, as a balanced totality and, on the other, as fragmented. And when one is presented, through a religious symbol, with a consciousness of this structure qua totality, one can be empowered to overcome estrangement.

What about the phenomena of anxiety and courage? Anxiety is the presence to consciousness of the threat of nonbeing, and courage is the conquest of that threat of nonbeing. But what is the source of courage if there is nothing beyond the self-world structure of consciousness in which the threat of nonbeing arises? Once again, one need only look to the self-world structure taken as a whole. The very existence of anxiety or nonbeing requires that nonbeing stands over against being, that is, that nonbeing is not alone but is juxtaposed to being in a whole encompassing them both. One cannot even make sense of the word *nonbeing* without reference to the word *being*; nonbeing, by definition, cannot exist alone but "is" only the negation of being. Thus, even as nonbeing counters being, the self-world structure transcends this moment of negation. Nonbeing, while it can negate a particular instance of being, cannot destroy the whole self-world structure, for that structure is a precondition for the negation of being. Courage, then, is an instance of empowerment resulting from an awareness of the self-world structure qua totality and its insulation from the threat of nonbeing.

Granted that the self-world structure of consciousness qua totality is *non*theistic (certainly it is not equivalent to the Supreme Being), can it be said to be *post*-theistic? The latter term suggests a dimension of reality that, in addition to being something other than the Supreme Being, is nonetheless a legitimate goal for the religious quest. One might affirm its post-theistic character by arguing that the self-world structure qua totality is the proper object of ultimate concern, for insofar as it serves as a source of empowerment—delivering humans from the threats of nonbeing, estrangement, and ambiguity—it determines human being and not being.

Both examples selected, the radicalization of Tillich's system toward transcendence and the radicalization of his system toward immanence, would of course have to be more fully developed before one could determine their actual viability. These examples do indicate, however, that the phenomenon of empowerment may be the key not only to Tillich's post-theistic interpretation of the Christian faith but also to the appropriation and adaptation of that interpretation in the present day. Attention to the place of empowerment may, in other words, allow one to take up the post-theistic component of Tillich's system without adopting his ontological speculations about being-itself.

Bibliography

Works by Tillich

Tillich, Paul. "An Afterword: Appreciation and Reply." In *Paul Tillich in Catholic Thought*. Rev. ed. Edited by Thomas F. O'Meara, OP, and Donald Weisser, OP, 369-80. Garden City NY: Image, 1969.

__________. *Biblical Religion and the Search for Ultimate Reality*. Chicago: University of Chicago Press, 1955.

__________. *Christianity and the Encounter of the World Religions*. New York: Columbia University Press, 1963.

__________. "Christianity and Other Faiths." *Union Seminary Quarterly Review* 20 (January 1965): 177-78.

__________. *The Courage to Be*. New Haven: Yale University Press, 1952.

__________. *Dynamics of Faith*. New York: Harper and Row, 1957.

__________. "Existential Analysis and Religious Symbols." In *Contemporary Problems in Religion*, edited by Harold A. Basilius, 35-55. Detroit: Wayne University Press, 1956.

__________. "The Fundamental Relationship Between Philosophy and Religion." In *Twentieth Century Theology in the Making*. Vol. 2, *The Theological Dialogue: Issues and Resources*, edited by Jaroslav Pelikan, 297-309. New York: Harper and Row, 1970.

__________________. *Gesammelte Werke.* 14 vols. Stuttgart: Evangelisches Verlagswerk, 1959-1974.

__________________. "The God Above God." *The Listener* 66 (3 August 1961): 169-72.

__________________. *The Interpretation of History.* Translated by N. A. Rasetzki and Elsa L. Talmey. New York: Scribner's, 1936.

__________________. "Interrogation of Paul Tillich." Conducted by William L. Reese. In *Philosophical Interrogations,* edited by Sydney Rome and Beatrice Rome, 355-409. New York: Holt, Rinehart and Winston, 1964.

__________________. *Love, Power, and Justice.* New York: Oxford University Press, 1954.

__________________. "The Meaning and Justification of Religious Symbols." In *Religious Experience and Truth,* edited by Sidney Hook, 3-11. New York: New York University Press, 1961.

__________________. *Morality and Beyond.* New York: Harper and Row, 1963.

__________________. "Myth and Mythology." In *Twentieth Century Theology in the Making.* Vol. 2, *The Theological Dialogue: Issues and Resources,* edited by Jaroslav Pelikan, 342-54. New York: Harper and Row, 1970.

__________________. "The Nature of Religious Language." In *Theology of Culture,* edited by Robert C. Kimball, 53-67. London: Oxford University Press, 1959.

__________________. *Political Expectation.* Edited by James Luther Adams. New York: Harper and Row, 1971. Reprint: Macon GA: Mercer University Press, 1981.

__________________. "The Problem of Theological Method." *Journal of Religion* 27 (January 1947): 16-26.

__________________. *The Protestant Era.* Abridged ed. Edited and translated by James Luther Adams. Chicago: University of Chicago Press, 1957.

__________________. "Rejoinder." *Journal of Religion* 46 (January 1966): 184-96.

__________________. "Relation of Metaphysics and Theology." *Review of Metaphysics* 10 (September 1956): 57-63.

__________________. "The Religious Symbol." In *Religious Experience and Truth,* edited by Sidney Hook, 301-21. New York: New York University Press, 1961.

__________________. "Reply to Interpretation and Criticism." In *The Theology of Paul Tillich.* 2d ed. Edited by Charles W. Kegley, 374-94. New York: Pilgrim Press, 1982.

__________. "Revelation and the Philosophy of Religion." In *Twentieth Century Theology in the Making.* Vol. 2, *The Theological Dialogue: Issues and Resources*, edited by Jaroslav Pelikan, 46-56. New York: Harper and Row, 1970.

__________. "The Significance of the History of Religions for the Systematic Theologian." In *The Future of Religions*, edited by Jerald C. Brauer, 80-94. Westport CT: Greenwood Press, 1976.

__________. "Symbol and Knowledge: A Response." *Journal of Liberal Religion* 2 (Spring 1941): 202-206.

__________. "Symbols of Eternal Life." *Harvard Divinity Bulletin* 26 (April 1962): 1-10.

__________. *Systematic Theology.* 3 vols. Chicago: University of Chicago Press, 1951-1963.

__________. "Theology and Symbolism." In *Religious Symbolism*, edited by F. Ernest Johnson, 107-16. New York: Harper, 1953.

__________. "The Two Types of Philosophy of Religion." In *Theology of Culture*, edited by Robert C. Kimball, 10-29. London: Oxford University Press, 1959.

__________. *Ultimate Concern: Tillich in Dialogue.* Edited by D. Mackenzie Brown. New York: Harper and Row, 1965.

__________. *What is Religion?* Edited by James Luther Adams. New York: Harper and Row, 1969.

__________. "The Word of God." In *Language: An Inquiry into its Meaning and Function*, edited by Ruth Nanda Anshen, 122-33. New York: Harper, 1957.

Other Works

Adams, James Luther. *Paul Tillich's Philosophy of Culture, Science and Religion.* New York: Harper and Row, 1965.

Aldwinckle, R. F. "Tillich's Theory of Religious Symbolism." *Canadian Journal of Theology* 10 (April 1964): 110-17.

Allen, Diogenes. "A Christian Theology of Other Faiths." *Theology Today* 38 (October 1981): 305-13.

Alston, William P. "Tillich on Idolatry." *Journal of Religion* 38 (October 1958): 263-67.

__________. "Tillich's Conception of a Religious Symbol." In *Religious Experience and Truth*, edited by Sidney Hook, 12-26. New York: New York University Press, 1961.

Altizer, Thomas J. J., and Hamilton, William. *Radical Theology and the Death of God*. Indianapolis: Bobbs-Merrill, 1966.

Aquinas, Thomas. *Summa Theologiae*. Edited by Thomas Gilby, OP. Vol. 1, part 1, questions 1-13. Garden City NY: Image, 1969.

Armbruster, Carl J., SJ. *The Vision of Paul Tillich*. New York: Sheed and Ward, 1967.

Aubrey, Edwin. "The Religious Symbol." *Journal of Liberal Religion* 2 (Spring 1941): 201-202.

Ayers, R. H. "Myth in Theological Discourse: A Profusion of Confusion." *Anglican Theological Review* 48 (April 1966): 200-17.

Bastian, H. D. *Theologie der Frage: Ideen zur Grundlegung einer theologischen Didaktik und zur Kommunikation der Kirchen der Gegenwart*. Munich: Chr. Kaiser Verlag, 1969.

Blanshard, Brand. "Symbolism." In *Religious Experience and Truth,* edited by Sidney Hook, 48-54. New York: New York University Press, 1961.

Bochenski, J. M., OP. "Some Problems for a Philosophy of Religion." In *Religious Experience and Truth,* edited by Sidney Hook, 39-47. New York: New York University Press, 1961.

Bowker, John W. "Can Differences Make a Difference? A Comment on Tillich's Proposals for Dialogue between Religions." *Journal of Theological Studies* 24 (April 1973): 158-88.

Brügmann, Veit. "Die Durchführung der Methode der Korrelation in den religiösen Reden Paul Tillichs." Ph.D. diss., University of Hamburg, 1969.

Bryan, Lawrence. *The Thought of Paul Tillich: A Select Bibliographical Companion to the Systematic Theology*. Evanston IL: Garrett Theological Seminary Library, 1973.

Burkle, Howard. "Tillich's 'Dynamic-Typological' Approach to the History of Religions." *Journal of the American Academy of Religion* 49 (June 1981): 175-85.

Burns, Robert, OP. "Paul Tillich and the World Religions." *Angelicum* 54 (1973): 394-416.

Bush, Richard C. "Frithjof Schuon's *The Transcendent Unity of Religions:* Con." *Journal of the American Academy of Religion* 44 (December 1976): 715-19.

Butchvarov, Panayot. *Being Qua Being: A Theory of Identity, Existence and Predication.* Bloomington: Indiana University Press, 1979.

Carey, John J. "Tillich Archives: A Bibliographical and Research Report." *Theology Today* 32 (April 1975): 46-55.

Chapey, Fernand. "Le principe de corrélation dans la théologie systématique de Paul Tillich." *Recherches de Science Religieuse* 59 (January-March 1971): 5-25.

Cherbonnier, E. "Biblical Metaphysics and Christian Philosophy." *Theology Today* 9 (October 1952): 360-75.

Christian, William A. *Oppositions of Religious Doctrines.* New York: Herder and Herder, 1972.

Clarke, Bowman L. "God and the Symbolic in Tillich." *Anglican Theological Review* 43 (July 1961): 302-11.

Clayton, John P. *The Concept of Correlation: Paul Tillich and the Possibility of a Mediating Theology.* Berlin: de Gruyter, 1980.

__________. "Dialektik und Apologetik in der theologischen Entwicklung Paul Tillichs." *Zeitschrift für Theologie und Kirche* 75 (1978): 213-32.

__________. "Questioning, Answering and Tillich's Concept of Correlation." In *Kairos and Logos: Studies in the Roots and Implications of Tillich's Theology,* edited by John J. Carey, 135-57. Cambridge MA: North American Paul Tillich Society, 1978. Reprint: Macon GA: Mercer University Press, 1984.

__________. "Was heisst 'Korrelation' bei Paul Tillich?" *Neue Zeitschrift für systematische Theologie und Religionsphilosophie* 20 (1978): 175-91.

__________. "Was ist falsch in der Korrelationstheologie?" *Neue Zeitschrift für systematische Theologie und Religionsphilosophie* 16 (1974): 93-111.

Cobb, John B. *Beyond Dialogue: Toward a Mutual Transformation of Christianity and Buddhism.* Philadelphia: Fortress Press, 1982.

__________. *Living Options in Protestant Theology: A Survey of Methods.* Philadelphia: Westminster, 1962.

Cox, Harvey. *The Secular City.* New York: Macmillan, 1965.

Daane, James. "Paul Tillich's *Systematic Theology.*" *Calvin Forum* 17 (December 1951): 79-83.

Dänzer, Hermann. "Der Begriff des Symbols in der Theologie Paul Tillichs und das physikalische Modell." *Physikalische Blätter* 19 (1963): 540-46.

Davis, Charles. *Christ and the World Religions.* London: Hodder and Stroughton, 1970.

Demos, Raphael. "Religious Symbols and/or Religious Beliefs." In *Religious Experience and Truth*, edited by Sidney Hook, 55-58. New York: New York University Press, 1961.

__________. "Tillich's Philosophical Theology." *Philosophy and Phenomenological Research* 19 (September 1958): 74-85.

Doyle, Dennis. "The Symbolic Element in Belief: An Alternative to Tillich." *Thomist* 45 (July 1981): 449-71.

Dreisbach, Donald F. "Paul Tillich's Doctrine of Religious Symbols." *Encounter* 37 (Autumn 1976): 326-43.

__________. "Paul Tillich's Hermeneutic." *Journal of the American Academy of Religion* 43 (March 1975): 84-94.

Dunne, John S. *The Way of All the Earth.* New York: Macmillan, 1972.

Dunphy, Jocelyn. *Paul Tillich et le symbole religieux.* Preface by Paul Ricoeur. Paris: J. P. Delarge, 1977.

__________. "Symbolique et symbole dans l'oeuvre de P. Tillich." *Études theologiques et religieuses* 53 (1978): 204-14.

Edwards, Paul. "Prof. Tillich's Confusions." *Mind* 74 (April 1965): 192-214.

Ehrlich, Leonard H. "Tillich's 'symbol' vis-à-vis Jasper's 'cipher.' " *Harvard Theological Review* 66 (January 1973): 153-56.

Emmet, Dorothy. "Paul Tillich's *Systematic Theology*." *Journal of Theological Studies* 4 (October 1953): 294-98.

Farley, Edward. "The Principle of Correlation: Transcendence and Theological Method." In *The Transcendence of God*, 97-102. Philadelphia: Westminster, 1960.

Fenton, John Y. "Being-itself and Religious Symbolism." *Journal of Religion* 45 (April 1965): 73-86.

Ferre, N. F. S. "Three Critical Issues in Tillich's Philosophical Theology." *Scottish Journal of Theology* 10 (September 1957): 225-38.

Ferrell, Donald R. "The Relationship of Philosophy and Theology in the Thought of Paul Tillich." Ph.D. diss., Graduate Theological Union, 1974.

Ford, Lewis S. "The Ontological Foundation of Paul Tillich's Theory of the Religious Symbol." Ph.D. diss., Yale University, 1963.

__________. "The Three Strands of Tillich's Theory of Religious Symbols." *Journal of Religion* 46 (January 1966): 104-30.

__________. "Tillich and Thomas: The Analogy of Being." *Journal of Religion* 46 (April 1966): 229-45.

__________. "Tillich's One Nonsymbolic Statement: A propos of a Recent Study by Rowe." *Journal of the American Academy of Religion* 38 (June 1970): 176-82.

Frege, Gottlob. "On Sense and Meaning." Translated by Max Black. In *Translations from the Philosophical Writings of Gottlob Frege*. 3d ed. Edited by Peter Geach and Max Black, 56-78. Totowa NJ: Rowman and Littlefield, 1980.

Frick, Eugene G. "The Meaning of Religion in the Religionswissenschaft of Joachim Wach, the Theology of Paul Tillich, and the Theology of Karl Rahner: An Inquiry into the Possibility of a Christian Theology of the History of Religions." Ph.D. diss., Marquette University, 1972.

Furuya, Yasuo Carl. "Apologetic or Kerygmatic Theology?" *Theology Today* 16 (January 1960): 471-80.

Gadamer, Hans-Georg. *Truth and Method*. Translation edited by Garrett Barden and John Cumming. New York: Continuum, 1975.

Gilkey, Langdon. *Naming the Whirlwind: The Renewal of God-Language*. 454-57. Indianapolis: Bobbs-Merrill, 1969.

__________. "The New Watershed in Theology." *Soundings* 64 (Summer 1981): 118-31.

__________. "Tillich: The Master of Mediation." In *The Theology of Paul Tillich*. 2d ed. Edited by Charles W. Kegley, 26-58. New York: Pilgrim Press, 1982.

Gollwitzer, Helmut. *The Existence of God as Confessed by Faith*. Translated by James W. Leitch. London: SCM, 1965.

Gragg, Alan. "Paul Tillich's Existential Questions and Their Theological Answers: A Compendium." *Journal of Bible and Religion* 34 (January 1966): 4-17.

Hamilton, Kenneth. "The New Dogma of Religious Symbolism: A Critique of the Viewpoints of Tillich and Jaspers." *Encounter* 25 (Summer 1964): 368-77.

__________. *The System and the Gospel: A Critique of Paul Tillich*. New York: Macmillan, 1963.

__________. "Tillich's Method of Correlation." *Canadian Journal of Theology* 5 (April 1959): 87-95.

Hammond, Guyton B. "Examination of Tillich's Method of Correlation." *Journal of Bible and Religion* 32 (July 1964): 248-51.

__________. *The Power of Self-Transcendence: An Introduction to the Philosophical Theology of Paul Tillich.* St. Louis: Bethany Press, 1966.

Harris, Ishmar. "The Dilemma of the Universal and the Particular Nature of Religion." *Journal of Religious Thought* 37 (Spring-Summer 1980): 42-49.

Hartmann, Walter, "Die Methode der Korrelation von philosophischen Fragen und theologischen Antworten bei Paul Tillich." Inaugural diss., University of Göttingen, 1954.

Hartshorne, Charles. "Tillich and the Non-Theological Meanings of Theological Terms." In *Paul Tillich: Retrospect and Future.* Introduction by T. A. Kantonen, 19-30. Nashville: Abingdon, 1966.

Heidegger, Martin. *Being and Time.* Translated by John Macquarrie and Edward Robinson. New York: Harper and Row, 1962.

__________. "What is Metaphysics?" Translated by R. F. C. Hull and Alan Crick. In *Existence and Being*, edited by Werner Brock, 325-61. Chicago: Henry Regnery, 1949.

Hick, John. *God Has Many Names: Britain's New Religious Pluralism.* London: Macmillan, 1980.

__________. "Towards a Philosophy of Religious Pluralism." *Neue Zeitschrift für systematische Theologie und Religionsphilosophie* 22 (1980): 131-49.

Holmer, Paul L. "Paul Tillich and the Language About God." *Journal of Religious Thought* 22 (1965-1966): 35-50.

__________. "Paul Tillich: Language and Meaning." *Journal of Religious Thought* 22 (1965-1966): 85-106.

Hook, Sidney. "The Atheism of Paul Tillich." In *Religious Experience and Truth*, edited by Sidney Hook, 59-64. New York: New York University Press, 1961.

Hopper, David. *Tillich: A Theological Portrait.* Philadelphia: J. B. Lippincott, 1967.

Horner, James. "Tillich's Rejection of Absolute Mysticism." *Journal of Religion* 58 (April 1978): 130-39.

Hume, David. *A Treatise of Human Nature.* 2 vols. London: J. M. Dent, 1964.

James, Robison B. "The Symbolic Knowledge of God in the Theology of Paul Tillich." Ph.D. diss., Duke University, 1965.

James, William. *The Varieties of Religious Experience.* Foreword by Jacques Barzun. New York: New American Library, 1958.

Johnson, Robert C. *Authority in Protestant Theology.* Philadelphia: Westminster, 1959.

Johnson, William A. "Tillich's Religious Symbol." *Encounter* 23 (Summer 1962): 325-42.

Johnson, W. G. "Martin Luther's Law-Gospel Distinction and Paul Tillich's Method of Correlation: A Study in Parallels." *Lutheran Quarterly* 23 (August 1971): 274-88.

Kaufman, Gordon D. "Can a Man Serve Two Masters?" *Theology Today* 15 (April 1958): 59-77.

Kaufmann, Walter. "Symbols: contra Tillich." In *Critique of Religion and Philosophy.* 189-96. Princeton: Princeton University Press, 1978.

Keefe, Donald J., SJ. *Thomism and the Ontological Theology of Paul Tillich: A Comparison of Systems.* Leiden: E. J. Brill, 1971.

Kelsey, David. *The Fabric of Paul Tillich's Theology.* New Haven: Yale University Press, 1967.

__________. *The Uses of Scripture in Recent Theology.* Philadelphia: Fortress Press, 1975.

Killen, R. Allan. *The Ontological Theology of Paul Tillich.* Kampen, Netherlands: J. H. Kok, 1956.

Knitter, Paul. "European Protestant and Catholic Approaches to the World Religions: Complements and Contrasts." *Journal of Ecumenical Studies* 12 (Winter 1975): 13-28.

__________. "What is German Protestant Theology Saying About the Non-Christian Religions?" *Neue Zeitschrift für systematische Theologie und Religionsphilosophie* 15 (1973): 38-64.

Kraemer, Hendrik. "A Criticism of Paul Tillich's 'Reconciliation.' " In *Religion and the Christian Faith.* 426-48. Philadelphia: Westminster, 1956.

Kriegstein, Matthias von. *Paul Tillichs Methode der Korrelation und Symbolbegriff.* Hildesheim: Gerstenberg, 1975.

Langford, Thomas A. "A Critical Analysis of Paul Tillich's Method of Correlation." Ph.D. diss., Duke University, 1958.

Lewis, Douglass. "The Conceptual Structure of Tillich's Method of Correlation." *Encounter* 28 (Summer 1967): 263-74.

Lipner, Julius. "Does Copernicus Help: Reflections for a Christian Theology of Religions." *Religious Studies* 13 (June 1977): 243-58.

Looff, Hans. *Der Symbolbegriff in der neueren Religionsphilosophie und Theologie.* Kant-Studien, supplement no. 69. Köln: Kölner Universitäts Verlag, 1955.

Loomer, Bernard. "Tillich's Theology of Correlation." *Journal of Religion* 36 (May 1956): 150-56.

McClean, George F., OMI. "Symbol and Analogy: Tillich and Thomas." In *Paul Tillich in Catholic Thought.* Rev. ed. Edited by Thomas F. O'Meara, OP, and Donald M. Weisser, OP, 195-246. Garden City NY: Image, 1969.

McDonald, H. D. "The Symbolic Theology of Paul Tillich." *Scottish Journal of Theology* 17 (December 1964): 414-30.

McKelway, Alexander J. *The Systematic Theology of Paul Tillich: A Review and Analysis.* Introduction by Karl Barth. Richmond: John Knox, 1964.

Macleod, Alistair M. *Paul Tillich: An Essay on the Role of Ontology in His Philosophical Theology.* London: George Allen and Unwin, 1973.

Mahan, Wayne. *Tillich's System.* San Antonio: Trinity University Press, 1974.

Martin, Bernard. *The Existentialist Theology of Paul Tillich.* New York: Bookman Associates, 1963.

__________. "Paul Tillich and Judaism." *Judaism* 15 (Spring 1966): 180-88.

Merritt, David R. "Tillich's Method of Correlation." *Reformed Theological Review* 21 (October 1962): 65-75.

Meynell, Hugo. "Tillich's Theological Method." In *The New Theology and Modern Theologians.* 137-56. London: Sheed and Ward, 1967.

Mondin, Battista. *The Principle of Analogy in Protestant and Catholic Theology.* The Hague: Martinus Nijhoff, 1963.

Morris, John S. "The Philosophical Basis of Tillich's Apologetic Theology." *Christian Scholar* 47 (Fall 1964): 233-42.

Nelson, John W. "Inquiry into the Methodological Structure of Paul Tillich's *Systematic Theology.*" *Encounter* 35 (Summer 1974): 171-83.

Nörenberg, Klaus-Dieter. *Analogia Imaginis: Der Symbolbegriff in der Theologie Paul Tillichs.* Gütersloh: Gütersloher Verlagshaus Gerd Mohn, 1966.

O'Connor, Edward. "Paul Tillich: An Impression." In *Paul Tillich in Catholic Thought.* Rev. ed. Edited by Thomas F. O'Meara, OP, and Donald M. Weisser, OP, 56-75. Garden City NY: Image, 1969.

Osborne, Kenan B. *New Being: A Study on the Relationship between Conditioned and Unconditioned Being According to Paul Tillich*. The Hague: Martinus Nijhoff, 1969.

Palmer, Michael. "Correlation and Ontology: A Study in Tillich's Christology." *Downside Review* 96 (April 1978): 120-31.

Panikkar, Raimundo. *The Intrareligious Dialogue*. New York: Paulist Press, 1978.

Partin, H. B. "Theology and History of Religions: Issues in Some Recent Literature." *Anglican Theological Review* 53 (October 1971): 170-78.

Petit, Jean-Claude. "La méthode de corrélation de Paul Tillich: quelques remarques." *Science et esprit* 26 (January-April 1974): 145-59.

Randall, John Herman, Jr. "The Ontology of Paul Tillich." In *The Theology of Paul Tillich*. 2d ed. Edited by Charles W. Kegley, 166-95. New York: Pilgrim Press, 1982.

Reese, William L. "Analogy, Symbolism, and Linguistic Analysis." *Review of Metaphysics* 13 (March 1960): 447-68.

Reisner, Erwin. "Die Frage der Philosophie und die Antwort der Theologie." *Zeitschrift für Theologie und Kirche* 53 (1956): 251-63.

Repp, Martin. "Zum Hintergrund von Paul Tillichs Korrelations-Methode." *Neue Zeitschrift für systematische Theologie und Religionsphilosophie* 24 (1982): 206-15.

Reymond, Bernard. "Symbol und Erkenntnis bei Tillich und Sabatier." *Neue Zeitschrift für systematische Theologie und Religionsphilosophie* 22 (1980): 211-21.

Rhein, Christoph. *Paul Tillich: Philosoph und Theologe*. Stuttgart: Evangelisches Verlagswerk, 1957.

Richard, Jean. "Symbolisme et analogie selon Paul Tillich." *Laval theologique et philosophique* 33 (1977): 183-202.

Ringleben, Joachim. "Paul Tillich's Theologie der Methode." *Neue Zeitschrift für systematische Theologie und Religionsphilosophie* 17 (1975): 246-68.

Robinson, John A. T. *Truth is Two-Eyed*. London: SCM, 1979.

Rosenthal, Klaus. "Myth and Symbol." *Scottish Journal of Theology* 18 (December 1965): 411-34.

Ross, Robert R. N., *The Non-Existence of God: Linguistic Paradox in Tillich's Thought*. New York: Edward Mellen Press, 1978.

Rowe, William L. *Religious Symbols and God: A Philosophical Study of Tillich's Theology*. Chicago: University of Chicago Press, 1968.

__________. "Tillich's Theory of Signs and Symbols." *Monist* 50 (October 1966): 593-610.

Santoni, R. E. "Symbolism and Ultimate Concern: A Problem." *Anglican Theological Review* 49 (January 1967): 90-94.

Scharlemann, Robert P. "Concepts, Symbols, and Sentences." *Theology Today* 22 (January 1966): 513-27.

__________. "Critical and Religious Consciousness: Some Reflections on the Question of Truth in the Philosophy of Religion." In *Kairos and Logos: Studies in the Roots and Implications of Tillich's Theology,* edited by John J. Carey, 74-95. Cambridge MA: North American Paul Tillich Society, 1978. Reprint: Macon GA: Mercer University Press, 1984.

__________. *Reflection and Doubt in the Thought of Paul Tillich.* New Haven: Yale University Press, 1969.

__________. "The Scope of Systematics: An Analysis of Tillich's Two Systems." *Journal of Religion* 48 (April 1968): 136-49.

__________. "Tillich's Method of Correlation: Two Proposed Revisions." *Journal of Religion* 46 (January 1966): 92-103.

Schillebeeckx, Edward. "Correlation Between Human Question and Christian Answer." In *The Understanding of Faith.* Translated by N. D. Smith, 78-101. New York: Seabury, 1974.

Schmitz, Josef. *Die apologetische Theologie Paul Tillichs.* Mainz: Matthias-Grünwald-Verlag, 1966.

Schneider-Flume, Gunda. " 'Entsprechungsdenken' and Sündenerkenntnis. Die Auswirkung der Methode der Korrelation auf das Sündenverständnis in der *Systematischen Theologie* Paul Tillichs." *Zeitschrift für Theologie und Kirche* 76 (1979): 489-513.

Schrader, Robert. *The Nature of Theological Argument: A Study of Paul Tillich.* Harvard Dissertations in Religion. Missoula MT: Scholars Press, 1975.

Schuon, Frithjof. *The Transcendent Unity of Religions.* Rev. ed. Translated by Peter Townsend. Introduction by Huston Smith. New York: Harper and Row, 1975.

Schwanz, Peter. "Das für Tillichs Methode der Korrelation grundlegende Problem der Vermittlung." *Neue Zeitschrift für systematische Theologie und Religionsphilosophie* 15 (1973) 254-71.

__________. "Ontologie oder transzendentaler Relationalismus? Die Fragwürdigkeit der Ontologie Tillichs." *Theologische Zeitschrift* 29 (1973): 419-27.

__________. "Zur neueren deutschsprachigen Literatur über Paul Tillich." *Verkündigung und Forschung* 24 (1979): 55-86.

Seigfried, Adam. *Das Neue Sein: Der Zentralbegriff der "ontologischen" Theologie Paul Tillichs in katholischer Sicht (Beiträge zur ökumenischen Theologie*, vol. 10). Munich: Max Hueber, 1974.

Sharpe, Eric J. "Christian Attitudes to Non-Christian Religions: A Bibliographical Survey." *Expository Times* 86 (March 1975): 168-71.

Simpson, Michael. "Paul Tillich: Symbolism and Objectivity." *Heythrop Journal* 8 (June 1967): 293-309.

Smart, Ninian. *Beyond Ideology: Religion and the Future of Western Civilization.* New York: Harper and Row, 1981.

Smith, Huston. *Forgotten Truth: The Primordial Tradition.* New York: Harper and Row, 1976.

__________. "Frithjof Schuon's *The Transcendent Unity of Religions*: Pro." *Journal of the American Academy of Religion* 44 (December 1976): 721-24.

__________. "Review of Tillich, Paul, *The Future of Religions.*" *Journal of Religion* 47 (April 1967): 184-85.

Smith, Wilfred Cantwell. *Questions of Religious Truth.* New York: Scribners, 1967.

__________. *Towards a World Theology: Faith and the Comparative History of Religion.* Philadelphia: Westminster, 1981.

Tait, L. Gordon. *The Promise of Tillich.* Philadelphia: Lippincott, 1971.

Tamaru, Noriyoshi. "Motiv und Struktur der Theologie Paul Tillichs." *Neue Zeitschrift für systematische Theologie und Religionsphilosophie* 3 (1961): 1-38.

Taubes, Jacob. "The Copernican Turn in Theology." In *Religious Experience and Truth,* edited by Sidney Hook, 70-75. New York: New York University Press, 1961.

__________. "On the Nature of the Theological Method: Some Reflections on the Methodological Principles of Tillich's Theology." *Journal of Religion* 34 (January 1954): 12-25.

Tavard, George H. *Paul Tillich and the Christian Message.* New York: Charles Scribner's Sons, 1962.

__________. "Paul Tillich's System." *Commonweal* 79 (7 February 1964): 566-68.

Thatcher, Adrian. *The Ontology of Paul Tillich.* New York: Oxford University Press, 1978.

Thomas, George F. "The Method and Structure of Paul Tillich's Theology." In *The Theology of Paul Tillich.* 2d ed. Edited by Charles Kegley, 120-39. New York: Pilgrim Press, 1982.

Thomas, J. Heywood. "The Correlation of Philosophy and Theology in Tillich's System." *London Quarterly and Holborn Review* 184 (January 1959): 47-54.

__________. *Paul Tillich: An Appraisal.* Philadelphia: Westminster, 1963.

Thomas, Terence. "On Another Boundary: Tillich's Encounter with World Religions." In *Theonomy and Autonomy: Studies in Paul Tillich's Engagement with Modern Culture,* edited by John J. Carey, 193-211. Macon GA: Mercer University Press, 1984.

Thomas, Vincent. "Darkness or Light?" In *Religious Experience and Truth,* edited by Sidney Hook, 76-82. New York: New York University Press, 1961.

Tracy, David. *Blessed Rage for Order: The New Pluralism in Theology.* New York: Seabury, 1975.

Urban, Wilbur. "Prof. Tillich's Theory of the Religious Symbol." *Journal of Liberal Religion* 2 (Summer 1940): 34-36.

Van Buren, Paul. "Tillich as Apologist." *Christian Century* 81 (5 February 1964): 177-79.

Van Hook, Jay M. "Paul Tillich's Conception of the Relation between Philosophy and Theology." Ph.D. diss., Columbia University, 1966.

Veatch, Henry. "Tillich's Distinction between Metaphysics and Theology." *Review of Metaphysics* 10 (March 1957): 529-33.

Weigel, Gustave, SJ. "Contemporaneous Protestantism and Paul Tillich." *Theological Studies* 11 (June 1950): 177-202.

__________. "Myth, Symbol and Analogy." In *Paul Tillich in Catholic Thought.* Rev. ed. Edited by Thomas F. O'Meara, OP, and Donald M. Weisser, OP, 241-55. Garden City NY: Image, 1969.

__________. "The Theological Significance of Paul Tillich." In *Paul Tillich in Catholic Thought.* Rev. ed. Edited by Thomas F. O'Meara, OP, and Donald M. Weisser, OP, 32-55. Garden City NY: Image, 1969.

Weischedel, Wilhelm. "Paul Tillichs philosophische Theologie: Ein ehrerbietiger Widerspruch." In *Der Spannungsbogen, Festgabe für P. Tillich zum 75. Geburstag,* edited by Karl Hennig, 25-47. Stuttgart: Evangelisches Verlagswerk, 1961.

Weiss, Paul. "Thank God, God's Not Impossible." In *Religious Experience and Truth,* edited by Sidney Hook, 83-89. New York: New York University Press, 1961.

Welch, Claude. "Paul Tillich and Theology of Correlation." In *Religion,* edited by Paul Ramsey, 249-59. Englewood Cliffs NJ: Prentice-Hall, 1965.

Whitson, Robley E. *The Coming Convergence of World Religions.* New York: Newman Press, 1971.

Wiebe, Paul. "The Theological Hermeneutics of Paul Tillich." Ph.D. diss., University of Chicago, 1975.

Yandell, Keith E. "On the Alleged Unity of All Religions." *Christian Scholar's Review* 6 (1976): 140-55.

Yonker, Nicholas. *God, Man and the Planetary Age: Preface for a Theistic Humanism.* Corvallis: Oregon State University Press, 1978.

Zabala, A. J. "Myth and Symbol: An Analysis of Myth and Symbol in Paul Tillich." Ph.D. diss., Institut Catholique de Paris, 1959.

Zaehner, Robert C. "Religious Truth." In *Truth and Dialogue: The Relationship between World Religions,* edited by John Hick, 1-19. London: Sheldon Press, 1974.

Zahrnt, Heinz. *The Question of God: Protestant Theology in the Twentieth Century.* Translated by R. A. Wilson. New York: Harcourt Brace Jovanovich, 1969.

Index

Adams, James Luther, 101
Aldwinckle, R. F., 20n57
Allen, Diogenes, 113n19
Alston, William P., 18, 20, 27, 71-72
Altizer, Thomas J. J., 96
Ambiguity, 9n21, 10, 28, 57-58, 61, 64, 79-83, 124
Aquinas, Thomas, 20-23
Aristotle, 12
Augustine, 2, 77n47

Being-itself, x, xiv-xv, 3, 5-29, 32, 37-41, 43-51, 53-60, 62, 64-73, 76-79, 81-86, 92, 99-100, 102-103, 111n16, 121-25, 127, 129-32. *See also* Depth
Bergson, Henri, 2
Böhme, Jacob, 2
Bowker, John W., 126n45
Bultmann, Rudolf, 102
Burkle, Howard, 112n18
Bush, Richard C., 114n22
Butchvarov, Panayot, 6n15

Christian, William A., 116n25
Clarke, Bowman L., 20n57

Clayton, John P., 60-61, 73, 97-98, 101, 102n118
Cobb, John B., 95n102, 113, 119-20
Correlation, explicit, apologetic method of, xv, 54, 60-63, 72, 84-86, 98-103; implicit, hermeneutical method of, xv, 54-103, 121-27
Cox, Harvey, 95

Davis, Charles, 113n19
Depth (of the structure of being), 12, 16, 28-29, 55, 59, 62-63, 76, 83n66, 83-87, 89-90, 98-99, 108, 122. *See also* Being-itself

Edwards, Paul, 18, 20
Empowerment, x-xv, 1, 9-13, 15, 26-29, 39, 41, 43-45, 49-51, 55-61, 66-67, 74, 76-83, 102-103, 105-106, 108, 122-25, 127, 129-32
Estrangement (Fallenness), 4, 9n21, 10, 28, 50-51, 58, 61, 64, 73-81, 88, 92, 94, 108, 126, 131

Fenton, John Y., 20n57
Ford, Lewis, 19-21, 23n67, 33n7, 35n14, 36n18
Frege, Gottlob, 32n5

Gadamer, Hans-Georg, 25, 36
Gilkey, Langdon, ix
God, ix-x, xiii-xv, 5, 16-18, 20-23, 38, 49, 57, 63-73, 78, 91-92, 95, 102, 105, 108, 115-18, 120, 122, 131-32. *See also* Symbol of God
Gollwitzer, Helmut, 22n65

Hamilton, Kenneth, 92-93, 98-99
Hammond, Guyton, 24n73, 71
Harris, Ishmar, 126n45
Hegel, G. W. F., x, 6, 8, 90, 93, 129-30
Heidegger, Martin, 2, 2n2, 9n23, 102
Hick, John, 114-16, 122
Hirsch, Emanuel, 102
Hook, Jay M. van, 87-88
Hook, Sidney, 20n57
Horner, James, 125n43
Hume, David, 8n17
Husserl, Edmund, xin4

Idealism, x, xv, 90, 129-31

James, William, xiii
Johnson, Robert C., 94
Johnson, William A., 20n57
Jung, Carl, 42n28

Kant, Immanuel, x, 3-4, 114-15
Kaufman, Gordon, 96
Kaufmann, Walter, 20n57
Kelsey, David H., 57
Kierkegaard, Søren, 16, 76, 93
Knitter, Paul, 113
Kraemer, Hendrik, 95n102
Kriegstein, Matthias von, 23n66, 96n107
Küng, Hans, 113

Lewis, Douglass, 88-89, 95n104
Lonergan, Bernard, x
Loomer, Bernard, 85-86
Luther, Martin, xiiin8, 77n47

Macleod, Alistair M., 56, 69n29
Martin, Bernard, 97, 126
McClean, George, 22
McDonald, H. D., 20n57
McKelway, Alexander, 93
Moltmann, Jürgen, 113
Mondin, Battista, 23n66
Morris, John, 97

Nietzsche, Friedrich, 12
Nonbeing, 2-7, 9, 13-15, 26, 28, 41, 51, 57, 61, 66-72, 75-76, 80, 92, 103, 130-32
Nörenberg, Klaus-Dieter, 23n66, 34n11, 37n18, 94

O'Connor, Edward, 23n66
Otto, Rudolph, 47-49

Palmer, Michael, 95n102
Panikkar, Raimundo, 118-19
Pannenberg, Wolfhart, 113
Paracelsus, P. A., 2
Paul, xiii, 83
Plato, 12

Rahner, Karl, 113
Randall, John Herman, xn3
Reese, William L., 20n57
Reisner, Erwin, 93
Repp, Martin, 90
Rhein, Christoph, 23n66
Richard, Jean, 22
Ringleben, Joachim, 90
Robinson, John A. T., 120
Rowe, William, 18n54

Scharlemann, Robert P., 19n54, 46n39, 55, 58n7, 63n13, 65n21, 85n70, 86-87, 89
Schelling, F. W., x, 2, 12, 125
Schillebeeckx, Edward, 95
Schleiermacher, F. D. E., 97
Schmitz, Josef, 22, 94
Schneider-Flume, Gunda, 94

Schopenhauer, Arthur, 2
Schuon, Frithjof, 114-16, 122
Schwanz, Peter, 90
Simpson, Michael, 23n66
Smart, Ninian, 120
Smith, Huston, 109n12, 114n22
Smith, Wilfred Cantwell, 116-18, 122-23
Structure of Being, xiv, 3-12, 20, 24, 26-29, 39, 41, 49-51, 55, 58-60, 62-63, 66-70, 74-77, 79-82, 84-91, 98-103, 109, 122-25, 130-32
Symbol, essential characteristics of, 31-43; functions of, x, 8-9, 14, 16-29, 32-35, 40-44, 69-73, 103, 105, 121-22, 127, 131; of the Christ, 16, 45-46, 53, 58, 63-64, 73-79, 83, 92, 103, 110-11; of God, ix, 27-28, 34, 38-40, 46, 51, 54, 58-59, 64-73, 74n41, 83, 103, 105, 129-30; of the Spirit, 64, 79-83, 103, 124; truth of, 44-51. *See also* Correlation

Tamaru, Noriyoshi, 89
Tavard, George, 97
Thatcher, Adrian, 80n58
Thomas, George F., 94
Thomas, Vincent, 20n57
Tracy, David, 96

Ultimate Concern, 14-17, 23-26, 28, 41, 44-45, 47-50, 69-70, 72, 103, 121-23, 132
Urban, Wilbur, 17, 20

Weigel, Gustave, 21n60, 22
Weischedel, Wilhelm, 96
Whitehead, Alfred North, x
Whitson, Robley, 120
Wittgenstein, Ludwig, 88, 95n104, 98
World Theology, Tillich's suggestions about, 105-12; Tillich's system and, xiv-xv, 105-106, 121-27; types of, 113-21

Zabala, A. J., 23n66
Zaehner, R. C., 113n19
Zahrnt, Heinz, 96

 *Symbol and Empowerment*

Designed by Alesa Jones
Composition by MUP Composition Department

Production specifications:
    text paper—60-pound Warren's Olde Style
    endpapers—Gainsborough Thistle
    covers (on .088 boards)—Holliston Kingston 35436 Natural Finish
    dust jacket—printed one color PMS 574
        on 80-pound Gainsborough Thistle

Printing (offset lithography) and binding
    by Penfield/Rowland Printing Company, Macon, Georgia